CW01661466

HAPPY ANYWAY

Jane Hanford

Dear Beth

I hope my little book teaches you how to be happy anyway

With love

Jane x

ISBN-978-1-8380903-3-3

Cover design by: Becky Hamblin

For Ben and Sam

CONTENTS

Introduction

This is the book I needed when I was a teenager, when I was tormented with very high levels of anxiety, a deep sense of unworthiness and was convinced that there was something wrong with me. Throughout most of my life, behind my surface level of normal behaviour was a morbid self-doubt that no amount of worldly success could fix. Nothing that happened out there could ever help because the problem lay inside.

Fortunately, even as a teenager some part of me remained optimistic that I could do something to help me to feel better. This optimism led me to study psychology and learn all that I could to improve the way I felt. After many years, two degrees, a lifetime of reading and more recently a study of Buddhist Psychology I have made that breakthrough. I don't want to keep it to myself. I now understand enough of the essence of how the mind works to make a real difference to others who are struggling like I struggled.

I have discovered that many themes overlap in different texts and across different disciplines, both ancient and modern. There are key learnings that have made sense to me and helped me. Each of the lessons in this book has been instrumental in my healing and development. Nothing here is new. Everything has been tried and tested within one or more of the schools of thought in modern psychology or across the eons of practice within the ancient traditions. More and more we see a coming together of the ancient and modern insights and techniques. This book condenses and brings together many of those ideas and practices.

I feel great sadness to see that we have an epidemic of mental health problems, across all parts of society, particularly amongst young people. I relate to their suffering and want to play a part in helping. The fact that there is little education for young people to help them to manage their emotional state and mental health is deeply distressing. I see that there is a lack of resources available for people when they are struggling with mental health difficulties, and an over reliance on medication as a solution. People need support, encouragement, validation and insight into their difficulties so they can find a way through and out. For most people this is ideally achieved with the help of a therapist, but this is not always available. In the gap between need and lack of resource I hope, through this book, I can help.

In more recent years I have coached very successful people who have shared in these intimate, confidential conversations their lack of self-belief. I believe that very many people secretly suffer from anxiety and lack of confidence and that these things don't go away on their own. I want to see younger people educated in how to manage their emotions and mental state so that they don't have to struggle their whole life with the anxiety of not feeling good enough.

In writing this book I have held in my mind and my heart my younger self. I know that these are the lessons that would have helped me then, and I hope will help anyone who feels that they share some of my earlier difficulties. I believe Carl Rogers when he wrote, "What is most personal is most universal". I hope that in writing this book, and sharing my understanding of what it is like to feel anxious and worthless, I can reach out to the hidden experience of others. I hope that people will feel understood and know that they are not alone. I also hope that the lessons I have learnt can help others of any age who struggle with anxiety to live more freely, more courageously and more happily.

To make this learning accessible to as many people as possible I have done away with references and academic jargon and tried to write in plain English. For those of you who want to find out more, I have provided a couple of references for most of the chapters, either people's names who have written on the subject or a psychological theory to look up, or sometimes a specific book that has been particularly helpful to me. It would be wonderful if this book could be a springboard for your ongoing journey of exploration towards greater peace and happiness.

The book is written as a number of short lessons. Each lesson will take just a couple of minutes to read. Try to allow each lesson a few moments, or days, to sink in. See if you can reach a deeper level of understanding. See if it finds resonance within. I hope each reader finds something that resonates, that opens and shifts. There is a progression through the lessons so you could read one at a time in sequence, but this is not strictly how it is meant to be read and each reader can find their own way through. Sometimes, I open a book off my shelf at random. I often find what I need at that time in those pages, so I offer that as a way into finding what you need.

This book does not make a claim on being a fix on its own and certainly not a quick fix. Rather it highlights some insights that will be helpful in understanding your mind and why it works the way it does. It will help you to understand that you are perfectly normal in thinking the way you do just because that is how human beings think. It will show you some gentle practices to help you see into your own mind and over time change how you think towards new ways that are more positive, more helpful and promote ongoing happiness. These practices and insights are always available whenever you remember them, and the more you use them, the better they work.

We all have a journey that beckons, a journey to awakening to your inner state of being, a journey towards self-awareness and self-mastery, a journey towards being in alignment with the world. As our society shuns talk of the inner experience and enlightenment some people never realise that there is a path to take and never start the journey inwards. By reading this book and others like it and by asking the important questions of life you are already started on the journey and that is the main thing - being on the journey to greater self-awareness and happiness. There is no destination, staying on the path is everything. Wherever you are on the journey it doesn't matter, staying on the path is everything. Dropping off the path is inevitable. Getting back on the path is everything. Don't give up. Don't go back. Stay on the path.

May you be safe, well and happy

Finding Stability

1 Finding Your Calm Inner Space

What is it like inside your head?

For most people thoughts are whirring round and round all of the time and negative thoughts have a stronger pull than positive thoughts. It is like a strong magnet pulling you towards the negative side of things and no matter how hard you try to think about something else your thoughts get pulled back into the vortex. It feels like a form of madness. Your mind does the thinking that causes you to feel unhappy. You don't want to feel unhappy but you find it difficult to control your thoughts.

It is important to realise that this is not just you. This is the way minds work when they are left to their own devices. So here's the rub, you cannot leave your mind to its own devices. You have to take charge. Now this is going to be hard. If it were easy we would all be doing it and there would be no more need for books like this, or therapists or medication for anxiety and so on. It is hard but you can take charge of your mind and your thoughts. You just need to dedicate yourself to the effort because it is absolutely worth it.

Try this. Wherever you are, just stop for a moment. Listen. What can you hear? What sounds are reaching your eardrums? Now listen again and stop before you label the sound. Stop before you imagine what the source of the sound is. Just simply allow the sound waves to hit your eardrums and focus on the sound itself. Close your eyes and hold this space in your head for a minute. Resist the normal impulse to label and know and just allow your sense of hearing to open wide and receive without your mind being involved, without any thoughts.

If that worked even for a split second, you have proven to yourself that there is a you behind your thoughts. When your thinking stops you are still there. You have just had a brief encounter with yourself. You have met yourself before but perhaps you didn't notice. In moments of calm or wonder, maybe on seeing something spectacular like a view or a sunset, or after a good cry, or after intense concentration and before your mind steps in and drives you to the next thing to think about or do.

This is your calm space, your source of inner peace. This is the place that you can return to whenever you need, where you can go whenever you feel stressed or unhappy, where you can rest and gather your strength. This is your home. When you practice stopping thinking on a regular basis, this sense of calm grows. The more you practice, the more it grows, until it becomes the inner space where you live, from which you interact with the world around you. This, after all, is you.

This is the place that grounds you, that gives you a sense of perspective on the thoughts that whirr around in your mind. As you practice you will start to see how your own mind works, how it obsesses, how it often thinks the worst, how sneaky it is at getting your attention. You can then begin to stop it, stop letting your mind have its way because it makes you miserable and start putting it to better use. There is so much to learn, so much to look forward to, so much fun to be had. How good it would be if your mind was occupied with these matters. How happy you could be.

2 Being Kind To Yourself

Developing an attitude of kindness towards yourself and others is essential if you want to be happy. Kindness will support you whatever difficulties you may face and kindness wishes for the best outcome for you and everyone else. In its full form, kindness means taking the action necessary to achieve that outcome. Kindness stops you judging yourself harshly which undermines your self-esteem and happiness, and stops you judging others harshly which only puts distance between you.

We live in a society that underrates kindness as though it is a weakness that leaves us vulnerable to manipulation. In taking this view we have created a society in which people are generally selfish and inward looking. We have lost the community and support that we evolved to be a part of and this causes us conflict. Deep down we feel alone and yearn for care and kindness. Sometimes we can find it difficult to find this kindness in others. Sometimes we can find it difficult to find it in ourselves. You have to break this rule and develop kindness if you want to be happy, and the first place to start is being kind to yourself.

To develop kindness you need to know what it feels like and practice this feeling so it becomes second nature. The easiest way to start is to think of someone who you feel a natural kindness for. It might be a pet or a child, someone you know well or someone you don't know well. Bring them into your mind as clearly as you can. Feel into the kindness that naturally wells up. Feel it in your body, in your heart. Take your time. Feel a softness, a tenderness, a welling up of love and kindness and hold yourself gently in this experience. Learn this feeling so you can recognise when it is there and when it isn't. Now direct this feeling towards yourself. Feel that warmth and gentleness and care directed towards yourself. Feel the kindness emanating from your heart turn back towards your own heart. Feel it surround you and cocoon you in loving kindness and relish this support, that you can give to yourself any time, all of the time. Know that you can take refuge in your own loving kindness whenever you want it and need it.

When you are kind to yourself you wish the best for yourself and you take the time to tend to your own needs and values. You don't compromise them with your own behaviour and you don't let other people trash your needs. You develop healthy boundaries to protect yourself as much as you need and want to. As you learn to respect yourself, others will learn to respect you. You do not push yourself beyond a point of healthy self-respect and you take rest when you need to. You also take on the challenges that will give life meaning for you, giving yourself time to learn and develop new skills and be patient with yourself while you learn, while you make mistakes. You take the time to become attuned to what makes you uncomfortable and act immediately when you need to preserve your safety and well-being. That includes your own negative thoughts as well as the speech and behaviour of others. As you practice kindness you stop the negative self-talk and you stop imagining what unkind thoughts other people are thinking about you.

Now you are ready to extend your kindness to others. It means looking at people you know with fresh eyes. Seeing them as separate people with their own needs. Listening and attending to them afresh and questioning, what do they need? How can you help them to meet their needs? Watch how they respond and how your relationships strengthen. It means meeting people that you don't know with a kindly appreciation, recognizing that they are just as real and whole as you are. Be quick to smile and slow to judge.

Practice this balancing act of kindness towards yourself and others. Try and bring it forward in your attitude and actions as much as you can. It is a foundation for your wellbeing and makes you happier. It helps you to build a network of friends and helps you to make the world a nicer place.

3 Using Your Breath To Find Stability

It's funny to think about the breath. Of course you are always breathing but you hardly ever think about it. It's only when you have to pay attention, like when you have a cough or you've run out of breath or you are under water. The rest of the time breath just happens without our awareness.

But when you pay attention to your breath it starts to become interesting because there is a link between your breath and your state of mind. When you are stressed and anxious your breath will be quick and shallow. It will happen quite naturally as your subconscious prepares you to fight or flee from danger. When you are more relaxed your breathing will naturally slow and deepen.

It also works in the other direction. Changing your breath changes your state of mind. You may already take a deep breath before you have to do something scary because you find it calms you down. By slowing your breath you can help to induce a more relaxed state of mind. By deliberately extending the out breath this works even better.

By using your imagination with your breath you can induce an even greater sense of calm. Imagine breathing in the things you want to keep and breathing out the things you want to lose. You can use your imagination with your breath to relax and lift your mood. Imagine breathing in a warm golden light; imagine it spreading to all parts of your body bringing calmness and happiness. When something good happens, for example someone pays you a compliment, instead of brushing it off, breathe it in and accept it with thanks. Breathe it in and let it become part of you. Imagine breathing out any feelings that you don't want to hold onto anymore. When you notice you are feeling anxiety, sadness or anger, try taking a deep breath and with your imagination scoop up the feeling and breathe it out and repeat until the strength of feeling subsides.

Simply keeping your attention on your breath is a way to steady the mind. You don't have to breathe in any special way, but just gently hold the attention there. Because the breath is always moving, it is a helpful focus for training the mind to be still. This simple focus on the breath is an ancient form of meditation still practiced the world over. As you stay with the in flow and out flow you learn to quiet the mind, you learn to manage your attention and you learn to tolerate boredom and discomfort. As you learn that you can easily tolerate boredom and discomfort you learn that you can face difficulties more easily, you learn to be resilient.

You will start to see your breath as a refuge in times of mental distress. Whenever you feel your anxiety starting to spiral out of control, switch your attention to your breath and try to deepen your breath. There is no need to panic. Your breath is always there to support you and to help you to manage your mental state.

Your breath is also there as an anchor to the present moment. When your mind is spinning off into its stories of failure and rejection, come back to the breath and the present moment. Right here, right now, everything is ok. You are ok. You are breathing and that is enough.

4 Being Present In Your Body

Maybe you don't think about your body very much, at least not in a kind way. You might be critical about the way your body looks as you compare it with everyone else's. In particular you compare it with models who are selected because they are exceptionally good looking. All you can get from comparing yourself with models is a sense of inadequacy.

When you came into existence you were born into this body, and this body will be with you from start to finish. You will be housed in this body your whole life. You might as well make friends with it. Can you appreciate how it holds you and carries you about? Can you thank your body for keeping you fairly pain free, even though you might take it for granted and don't treat it well? Can you be a kind friend to your body because after all, you are in it together for life? Can you look after it and tend to its needs because it needs you as much as you need it? Can you even marvel at what an incredible piece of work your body is? How intricately it balances your temperature, your blood chemistry, your breathing? How your kidneys filter your blood, how you grow, how your muscles and nerves respond to your wishes? Can you praise it and promise to take care of it your whole life? Because your body is your life.

Everything that makes life worth living is physical. The warmth of the sun on your skin, the touch of someone you care about, the tastes you love, the sounds of sea, of music, of birds. Pleasure is based in your senses. Without sensual pleasure life would be drab and unbearable. Ground your attention in your senses to find the pleasure in life. Be deeply grateful to your body for making life worth living.

Your emotions are felt in the body. When you feel sad you might feel a heavy weight on your chest, and the pit of your stomach feels like a stone. When you feel happy your heart feels light and fluttery. Nervousness often feels like butterflies in the stomach. Fear might make the blood drain from your extremities so your face and hands feel cold. Anger often makes you hot. Without these bodily responses to emotions you wouldn't know how you felt about things. This might seem strange because emotions are quickly taken up with thoughts about how you feel and so emotions seem to be in your head rather than in your body. But if you didn't have the physical sensations that go along with emotions you wouldn't know how you felt, and you would feel barely alive.

In fact you probably spend the great majority of time living in your head, thinking, planning, interpreting, judging and so on. This is very common, but is an odd way to live because it means that you are not fully alive in the present, in contact with your body and its senses and sensations. You might only be consciously aware of how you feel once a physical sensation becomes too acute to ignore, at which point you might even chastise your body for interrupting you.

We tend to believe that our head is in charge of everything and the body is a slave to making our conscious needs and desires come true. Yes you have plans and ambitions that you will need your body to support. But dig a little deeper and you might find that it is your body that is really running the show. You might want success in life so that you can live a life of comfort and ease (for your body) or so you can feel respected, supported and safe (for your body). You might find that the activities you choose make your body feel good. Choose wisely though because some activities that feel good in the short term are harmful in the long term, and harming your body will always end in misery. There is nothing so detrimental to your happiness as physical pain or disease.

On a day to day basis, your physical body and its processes largely dictate your behaviour. Hormones might lead you to feel irritable and snap at someone. If you are tired, everyday tasks can feel overwhelming and you are forced to rest. A boost of energy will spur you into an activity that you had been putting off. Needing food, drink or the toilet will radically change your behaviour until these needs are satisfied. Practice being more attentive to your body's needs so you learn how to nourish, exercise, rest and care for it. Looking after your body will be a great help in feeling better about yourself.

Be attentive to what is going on at an emotional level, how you are feeling and when you are triggered. All of this is information that will guide you through your day, helping you to deepen connections and make decisions that are right for you. Tuning into your body, its needs, rhythms and its moment-by-moment state, with friendliness, will make life run much more smoothly for you. Ignoring your body is ignoring yourself, your pleasure and your happiness.

5 Being Present In The Moment

Did you notice that right here, right now, in this very split second, you are ok and everything is ok? Start from this simple fact here and now and keep noticing it each moment until you come to realise that it is always true. This full awareness of the present moment is a secret gateway out of suffering that has always been available but you just couldn't see it when your mind was busy.

Bring your attention to this present moment. Try it now. Stop and look about you. What can you see? What can you hear? How are you feeling? Try not to label or judge anything, simply be wide eyed and take in the sights. Notice the colours, shapes and movement of things. Open your ears wide open to take in the sounds, the notes, the quality of the sounds, the music that it makes. How is your internal environment? Are you feeling restless, bored, anxious, relaxed? No judging.

When you are not judging, don't you find everything is just as it should be? Sink into the moment knowing that everything is just as it should be and rest here, in this moment, where all is well.

This is a place you can come to at any time. You can park your troubles and worries for a moment and come to this present moment. See the beauty around you. Even on a grey wet day you can look at the beauty of the raindrops and the puddles. You can always look at the sky and see the colours and shapes of the clouds.

Try to bring a sense of wonder and gratitude to what you witness. Be grateful for the rain and all of the benefits it brings to the land. Marvel at how this planet managed to hold so much water as it spins through the universe, enabling life to form and you to be here. Use the doorway of this moment to plug yourself into the wonder of the universe and the miracle that you are here at all.

While you rest in this moment, open to all your senses and feelings, you can relax your grip on things. You are not in charge of what is happening in the world and you don't have to hold on or struggle for things to turn out a certain way. Right now you don't even have to hope, you can just relax deeply and be with what is. Whatever you are feeling inside is just a part of being a human being, so you can simply observe what is going on, without taking responsibility or fighting the feeling. Accept your inner world with open kindness and rest with whatever is going on.

Remind yourself that the world has a place for you, that you are welcome in this world. And it doesn't need anything from you. You can relax and you will still be welcome.

6 How To Meditate

Across the world for thousands of years meditation has been at the heart of many spiritual traditions. In the last 150 years modern psychology has highlighted the value of self-awareness through quiet introspection or contemplation. More recently, through neuroscience and other scientific enquiry, the practice of meditation has been found to be deeply beneficial for mental health. In summary, meditation is almost universally recognised as the most valuable practice for developing mental health and happiness.

In its essence meditation is simply the act of sitting quietly. It is the quality of the quietness that makes it different from just sitting down in normal everyday life. In meditation you are training the mind to be quiet. This is harder than it sounds. Try it now. Set a timer for three minutes and sit comfortably with a quiet mind. Whenever a thought pops into your mind allow it to fade and return to your quiet mind.... How many times in three minutes did you have to return your mind to its calm state? Or did you get transported away and into your thoughts? This is what normally happens. This is why it is harder than it sounds and why it takes practice. It is called a practice because the more you do it the easier it will be for you to deliberately quiet and still the mind.

It helps to have a focus and the breath is readily available and a good place to start. The idea is to rest your attention on the breath, rather than strain to focus. As you breathe relax the body and mind and rest in the breath for a few minutes. Let your whole being be absorbed with the breath coming in and going out. Just that.

When thoughts pop into your mind, as they will, just let them go and return your attention to the breath. Notice how your mind tries to grab your attention and pull you away. As emotional and physical feelings arise, acknowledge them with kindness and return your attention to your breath. Accept all thoughts and feelings with a friendly welcome, trying not to judge any as good or bad, comfortable or uncomfortable. Try not to follow thoughts or feelings or get carried away with their stories, but gently observe their existence and return your attention to your breath. Your breath is your centre and your safe haven, where you can always go for rest.

Sometimes in the silent space that meditation allows, difficult thoughts, memories, emotions or physical distress can appear, making it impossible to maintain a quiet focus on the breath. Try to stay with these feelings for a little while, relaxing and accepting them as a natural part of human existence. This is where you learn about how to be with your difficult feelings so that they can loosen their grip on you. If they become unbearable it is better to break with the sitting practice. You might calm your mind by deepening the breath and resting there. Or you could try taking a walk. While you walk focus your attention on the input from all your senses, focus on the feeling of your feet touching the ground, the swinging of your legs and hips, the breath entering your lungs, the air as it moves against your skin. Notice the sights and sounds around you as if seeing or hearing them for the first time. In this way your mind can rest in the present while you are walking.

This may help to pave the way to a more peaceful state where you can resume a sitting meditation in the future. If your distress does not ease, please seek help from a trained professional who can lead you out of your traumatised thoughts and emotions to a place where you can feel safe again.

There are many forms of meditation, from ancient to modern. Some are part of a wider tradition or faith and some are standalone practices. Do some research and find the type that suits you so that you can keep the practice going.

When you are able to practice short spells of sitting or walking meditation, try to do this on a regular basis. In time you will notice huge benefits such as a clearer mind, a feeling of being calm and centred and more alive. A few minutes every day, early in the morning is best as it sets the tone for the day ahead. And throughout the day when difficulties arise take a moment to focus your attention and regain your calmness. As you continue your practice you will find it becomes more and more easy to stay calm and centred whatever difficulties you face. This simple practice will change everything for the better.

Learning About Being A Human Being

7 Why It's Not Easy Being A Human Being

The truth is that it's hard being a human being. You are not alone. We have a complex range of feelings and our intelligence is dazzling. As a species we have solved many of the mysteries of life, yet as individuals we find it frustratingly difficult to peer into the depths of our own mind and end our own suffering. We are not optimised to be happy.

At birth we are pretty happy as long as our basic needs are met. From birth onwards we start to learn about what we have to do to be comfortable, fed, clean and nurtured, what works and what doesn't. As we grow our needs grow and these lessons multiply until our inner world becomes unfathomably complex and the origins of our needs and feelings are lost to us. We muddle through with the business of being in the world continuing to learn and fine-tune our behaviour, whilst most of the fundamental lessons are taken as given.

Some of these lessons are positive. We might learn that we are generally likeable and capable. This belief sets a firm foundation for thriving and setbacks can be easily overcome. Some lessons are negative. We might learn that if we make a fuss people are likely to ignore us or hurt us. This could make us less likely to draw attention to ourselves and less able to communicate our needs. We might become fearful and anxious or aggressive as a way of coping. These early lessons become our unconscious blueprint for life. They inform us of what we are like and how the world works and responds to us. We take them for reality. It doesn't mean they are true.

Sadly, as a species, we are primed to respond to negative experiences. They outweigh the positive in the focus of our minds. Early negative experiences don't go away, they remain buried in our subconscious and often become an ongoing source of difficult emotions. We find it a challenge to change our emotional response because the roots are deeply buried and forgotten. No one has a perfect experience of life, and everyone has some level of suffering. You are not alone.

So you see how the way you feel and react to situations is not your fault. You had the experiences you had, and you learnt how best to respond, with the faulty equipment you have as a human being.

Many people go through their whole life unable to see the root cause of their suffering, never understanding that the impact of these early lessons and their learned response is hurting them. No one has shown them how to look inside or told them that it can be different. The truth is that you can learn and you can change, even at this fundamental level. Making the effort to learn and change is the difference between growing old and growing up.

Growing up as human being means more than aging. It means growing in self-awareness and self-control, growing in consciousness of who you are and what you are here for. It means delving into your own being, unpicking the threads of your emotions and your habitual reactions. It means allowing all emotions and accepting all thoughts, then sifting through to see what is helpful to you and what is not and applying yourself to the patient and persistent task of change for good. This is the process of becoming a grown up human being. This process is the pathway to happiness.

When people are content with themselves they have no need to hurt anyone else. People inflict pain on each other as a means of escaping the pain they feel inside. If that is right then the most important thing we can do to free ourselves from suffering, to be as happy as we can, and to help other people find their way to happiness. If that is right finding happiness is the most important job we have as human beings.

8 How Evolution Made You This Way

Human beings, as a species, are aware of our extraordinary intelligence. We believe that we have the ability to control our thoughts and behaviours. Our minds are always busy fixing and solving and generally creating a feeling of being in charge. It is easy to forget that human beings, including our minds, are a product of a long evolution. It is 4 billion years since life formed on this planet and 160 million years since the first mammal evolved. So by the time we get to modern humans 250,000 years ago a massive genetic blueprint had already been laid down.

If you accept that the purpose of evolution is survival then it follows that we have been built physically and mentally to survive. Essentially this means moving towards food, shelter and a mate, and moving away from threat of harm. Of these, it is more important to survival to move away from harm - fast.

So it makes perfect sense that our brain and nerves are wired to detect and react to threat first and foremost. This wiring has kept us alive as a species and allowed you to be alive today. It becomes clear then that fear and anxiety are inbuilt mechanisms and take first place in the way we react to the world around us. When we became humans this did not change.

Evolution is lazy, it takes the easiest, most efficient path to adding new features such as intelligence. If you look at the structure of the human brain, there is a new part, the bit that is uniquely human, which is called the cerebral cortex, wrapped around the old brain, which is still there inside, just as it was when we were early mammals. The new part is where higher intelligence is located, the part that allows us to solve problems, gives us language, social intelligence and so on. It was an easier job for evolution to make this outside part of the brain bigger in order to evolve greater intelligence, rather than integrating it fully into the whole.

Now the older part of the brain is still reacting to everything as either good (food, shelter, mate) or bad (threat). The problem is that this part of the brain has remained largely subconscious and we can't see into it. In evolutionary terms it wasn't necessary to give us insight into the workings of the mind to keep us alive. So the older part of the brain is constantly working below our conscious awareness, driving our reactions and outside of our control. It sends up messages of desire and threat to the conscious mind, which then has to decipher what the opportunity or threat is in this situation. The conscious mind has a challenge to maintain its impression of being in charge when it has an unseen, unknown, unpredictable and irresistible puppet master. It does this by keeping you constantly busy thinking so that you never have time to stop and question it.

As an example, you might be in a social gathering and you feel anxious because your unconscious mind has picked up some unfriendly body language. You feel the anxiety and look around the room and suddenly it feels less welcoming, you feel less accepted and more exposed. Your conscious mind will rationalise this by conjuring up stories about you, your deficiencies, your history of social mishaps and so on to pretend that these are the reasons for your anxiety. You are left feeling miserable and inadequate without knowing the real reason why.

Because the conscious mind makes sure it is always busy, sometimes it ignores or misses valuable messages coming up from the subconscious.

You could be busy trying to fit in and be liked and you push aside a nagging feeling that something or someone isn't safe. It is better to pay attention to these feelings and bring it up for consideration. Why am I feeling uneasy? Is this a situation I need to get out of? If you could peer into your subconscious mind and see how it works you could judge when it is giving you useful information and when it is over-reacting. Because of the way the brain has been constructed, it is not easy, but it is possible to get better. You do have an early warning system - you can pay close attention to your emotions.

All emotions originate in the subconscious mind, in the parts of the brain that evolved before we became human beings. Emotions are natural and unavoidable. How you respond to your emotions is within your control. If you pay close attention to your feelings, just as they emerge, and before you get carried away, you can quickly see if they are helpful or not. You can then decide what is the best course of action. It may be a deep breath to calm down or it may be a hasty exit. Staying aware of your constantly changing emotional state is a very important practice. Being able to observe your emotions, without reacting, is how you gain control of your emotions and your mental state. This is how you avoid getting caught up in anger, sadness and anxiety and how you cultivate calmness and happiness. This is how you personally evolve.

9 How Your Early Life Has Shaped You

We gain our fundamental understanding of ourselves and the world around us at a very early age. As newborn babies our needs are fairly simple. We need to be fed, clean, warm and comfortable. We need loving human interaction. When our needs are met we are content. When our needs are not met we are unhappy and we communicate our needs by crying so that our carers respond and meet our needs so we are happy again. But this doesn't always happen. If as a baby we cry and no one comes, our life is in danger. This is the gap where we learn to be scared.

With our limited physical capabilities and partly formed brain we have few options. If crying doesn't work we might save our energy and stop crying and wait it out. At a fundamental level we have learnt that asking others for what we need is pointless and we learn to shut down instead. Or we might cry harder and louder until someone does come and feed or change us. These responses form early connections in our developing brain and remain below our conscious awareness as blueprints for what to expect from other people and how we should behave.

If we learnt to shut down, we form a pattern where we don't expect people to help us. We hide our needs as something shameful and find it hard to ask for help. We might shield or withdraw from other people, or push them away to prevent the hurt and rejection we fear so much. We might try to suppress or numb the need we feel because it is too painful. These patterns of expectations and behaviours get reinforced and strengthened and without us knowing, they become the way we do things, they become 'us'.

If we learnt to cry harder and louder we can develop a pattern of acting up and demanding attention as we grow up. We might show up as brash, selfish and insensitive as we feel that our own needs are paramount and others' needs are not recognised or prioritised. We get angry with people when they can't do what we want. As we push people away, no one will get close enough to help us or tell us that there is a different, better way to behave.

We don't consciously realise our pattern as something that we can challenge. We simply accept it as the truth because these lessons were learnt so early when we were babies or infants and before our brains had a chance to develop critical thinking. We accepted the world around us, and the behaviour of others, particularly our parents or carers, as how things are. We learnt how we are from their reactions to us. If they were attentive, warm and caring we learnt that we are important and are more likely to grow up with a high level of self-worth. We recognise our needs and find healthy ways to meet them. If we were treated with physical or emotional cruelty or neglect we learnt that we are not important, or that we are bad. But this cannot be true. As a baby you couldn't possibly have been the cause of cruelty or neglect. There was never anything wrong with you. There is nothing wrong with you now. There is just that thought, that belief, buried deep, that you are not ok. This deep-seated belief robs you of your confidence and joy. Now you must dig deep to uncover and unlearn, and when you see that none of this is true you will be free to be happy just the way you are.

Note: I want to make it clear that parenting is difficult, and there is no such thing as perfect parenting. Even the most attentive parent will miss something that the child needs. Many parents in our society face significant challenges on top of the task of parenting. This is not a blame game. Most parents do the best they can. It's not easy.

10 Being You

You know yourself. You know your opinions, your likes and dislikes and your memories that make up the story of your life so far. You have a personality and habits that consistently define who you are.

You have good day and bad days. On good days you remember more of the things in your past that have gone well. Your achievements, your dear friends, your luck are all highlighted in your memory bank. Your outlook is optimistic and you enjoy the day so you are more likely to engage in activities and try new things. You are less upset by minor frustrations and find it easier to laugh at mishaps. On bad days your memory selects the failures and limitations from your past. You dwell on your misfortunes and expect the worst from life and other people. You are less likely to engage in activities or relationships as your energy drops and it becomes too much effort. It can take very little to switch you from one mood to the other.

You also have a range of moods or modes that

take over your state of mind. There are very many of them, each with their own values, agendas, feelings and needs. Here are a few you might recognise. The helping you comes to the fore when someone shows you they need your help. In this mode you feel a sense of competence, value and gratification from being useful to someone else. In contrast, when the jealous you takes over you are swept away with feelings of anger and pain and your thoughts obsess about the details of the hurt that has been caused or might be caused. Thoughts of revenge might rise up. When your inner victim takes over you blame others and external factors for your situation and won't take responsibility for the way things are. Anger and resentment are turned towards others and you stop looking for positive ways forward.

Some modes may be hidden. They come from early experiences that are forgotten and suppressed. You might find that there are some emotions that you know about but you can't feel. If a family doesn't express or tolerate the expression of anger, this emotion gets buried deep inside the child. Instead of feeling angry the mind converts it into a safer feeling, like sadness or confusion. If your mind goes foggy or panicked when conflict arises it could be that you are batting down a feeling of anger. Sometimes within a family environment any expression of sadness is disapproved of and seen as weak. This leaves a child with an inability to express sadness and so they may avoid emotional situations or getting too close to others because vulnerability is seen as a weakness.

The truth is we all have a full range of human feelings, emotions and personalities within us. We are all capable of being strong and positive, vulnerable, power crazed and cruel or passionate and loving and everything in between. When one or other of these states rise to the fore we feel differently, we behave differently; we become in effect a different person. Allow yourself to feel whatever you feel. All of it. It all has a place within you. Don't cling to the notion that you have to be consistent. Your feelings and emotional states change throughout each day. Allow them all. The only thing you need to manage is your behaviour so that you don't hurt yourself or others. All of the thoughts and feelings that go on inside of you, and all of the ways they change from day to day, are completely normal and completely human.

11 Being Human Is Enough

Imagine for a moment that you have enough of everything, that no matter what, you will always have enough and that you yourself are enough in every way. Sit with that thought for a moment and let it sink in. How does it feel? Does it feel as though you can relax and let go of the struggle to achieve and change and improve? What if it was true? What would life be like if you could hold onto that feeling?

Bring your thoughts to this very moment. As you sit here reading this page do you have everything you need, just for now? Are you safe, warm enough, not too hungry or thirsty, not in great discomfort? If that is the case then you have enough in this moment. And every moment that you can run through this checklist and answer yes to all the items you are proving to yourself that you have enough. If most of your life is spent in safety and shelter, without pain and with enough to eat and drink then you are truly lucky. The path to being happy is to live with the daily awareness of and gratitude for this blessing.

Throughout every day pay attention to the little rewards, the small satisfactions and achievements; the food and drink, the friendly conversation, the work that has gone well, the exercise you have taken. Take time to appreciate your safety, your wellbeing, your health. Appreciate yourself, remembering that you are doing your best and that is enough. Practice the habit of focusing on what you have rather than what you lack.

Being ok with who you are means rebelling against the society that teaches you the opposite: that you are not enough, that you are not competent, or successful enough, that you do not have the things that make you worthy. This means rewriting the script that people have been telling you all your life, the script that tells you that you need to struggle and strive, that you need to fit in and that you are not good enough as you are. This means actively cultivating the beliefs that you are enough and that you have enough.

Everyone is born equal. Every baby that enters the world, at that moment of birth has the same potential. The situations that babies are born into can be safe and nurturing or harsh and hostile. We may be born healthy or with physical or mental difficulties. We may be born into wealth or poverty. Each baby is either fortunate or unfortunate in its circumstances but the baby itself is not to blame. We may grow to be supported and educated or not, and so we may be better or worse at making good decisions. The point is that our circumstances vary widely but our inner being is the same and is equal. You are equal to everyone – the homeless person begging on the streets and the person ruling the country. Know that you can look each one in the eye as an equal. This means that no one is better or worse than you and we are all enough.

You are fortunate to be born in these times when for most of the population of the world there is enough to go round. Whilst the degree of inequality is shameful, there is still enough for most of us. Yet you tend to focus on what you are lacking. A lack of money, of time, of sleep, of approval, of love, of fun... the list goes on. Your mind is preoccupied with lack when you could focus instead on what you already have. Make a list of what you have and take nothing for granted. Start off from absolutely nothing and build your list. You have this book, a chair, a toothbrush, a room, a school, a friend, each friend, water to drink, a toilet that flushes ... Soon you will realise how full your life is. Add your experiences. A film you love, a meal you enjoyed, a trip to the beach, music you enjoy, conversations, praise, comfort ... Add in your strengths and talents. Your kindness, your intelligence, your sense of humour, everything that you are good at, everything you are learning …

How many pages do you need? This is the list you need to keep in the forefront of your mind. This is how you rewrite your script.

You don't need to compete with anyone because you have enough. You don't need to compare yourself with anyone because you are enough.

12 Being Happy

You are here to be happy, what else is there? Too often we lose sight of this simple goal. Your existence started from the beginning of the universe, through the eons of evolution, the chance of your ancestors meeting and having children, through the miracle of the survival of thousands of individuals through to the miracle of you being here. And here you are. The universe has worked very hard to make you. What is the point of all of that if you are to be miserable?

You can be confident that happiness is right because it is the best feeling, the one we want to feel more of, and because happiness is contagious. When you are happy you automatically pass on that good feeling, it makes you want to share it. It is very difficult to help others to feel happy if you don't feel happy yourself. Happiness is a force for good and something to be cultivated.

The trouble is that we pick up beliefs that take us away from this simple truth. Beliefs such as we should think of other people's happiness rather than our own. Or being good, wealthy and hard working is more important than being happy. Or we believe that we are not good enough or not worthy of being happy. Achieving happiness then requires work in dropping these beliefs so that we can regain the happiness that we had and lost.

Happiness is your natural state of being before you acquired these beliefs. In your natural state, provided your basic needs of food, shelter and comfort are met, contentedness just happens. But you are taught that this is not enough. You live in a society that constantly pesters you to want more, to achieve more, to be more. Because you buy into this myth, you believe that you don't have enough, that you need more to be happy. You are preoccupied with thoughts of not being enough or not having enough. You are caught up in this rat race like everyone else. You need to see through it and free yourself from it. In our society happiness is an act of rebellion.

It is hard to disentangle from these beliefs because they are strongly held. You think yes but I need to be smarter to make a living so I can have a nice lifestyle; yes but I have to be more attractive so that people like me; yes but I have to show my family how successful I am. These are all made up beliefs. You don't really need any of these. Society has drummed them into you and it is hard to free yourself from these myths but you have to try so that you can be happy.

The truth is that happiness is a choice. Happiness doesn't come from out there, it is not attached to any thing you can buy, any achievement you can attain. If you chase happiness out there you will never find it no matter how far you get. You can make your million but you still won't be happy. You will look amazing and have many friends but you still won't be happy. And because you are not happy you will think that it's because you haven't got enough, and you will want more, forever. Instead, turn around and look inside, rip out any thoughts of not being enough or not having enough and you will find that you can be happy right here and now, with whatever you have.

Ask yourself what do you really need. What are the basics that will carry you from one day to the next? You will be surprised by how little that is. If you believe that this is enough you can be happy, just like that.

Happiness is an option that you can choose at any moment. Try this. Imagine you are happy. Right here, right now go inside and conjure up a feeling of happiness. Feel it grow bigger and intensify. Close your eyes for a minute and revel in this feeling. There it is. Whenever you want to, you can just be happy. Practice this until you find it's your normal state of being. Happiness is a mindset. Happiness is a practice. Happiness is a choice.

Letting Go Of What Hurts You

13 Letting Go Of Trying To Be Perfect

The society we live in sets impossible ideals and then judges each and every one of us according to those ideals. We are all influenced by the media and people around us, and so we absorb and uphold these standards and judge ourselves and each other accordingly. Society presents us with a reflection that highlights our flaws and inadequacies, it judges us and finds us lacking at every level. We are trained to focus on our flaws and the flaws in others. Flaws are the currency of social interaction. We display our acceptable flaws to make ourselves more likeable. We hide our unacceptable flaws to stop being rejected. Society clouds our minds with negative judgments and we make ourselves and everyone else miserable with a general sense of inadequacy.

Some people are genetically blessed with looks

that are closer to society's ideals. They haven't worked for it and this is nothing to be admired. Some people focus on improving their looks at the expense of developing as a person and again this is no real cause for admiration. Some people are clever in one area or another. Some people achieve great wealth. Some people are famous. Some people are just lucky. Sometimes these people are held up as examples of what it means to be perfect so that we can all compare ourselves with these few and find ourselves lacking. However the reality of their day-to-day lives is much like yours and mine. They have lots of mundane things to do, they get bored and they doubt themselves.

Imagine a different world. Imagine a perfect world for you to be in. Just for a moment imagine that you are alone in a beautiful forest and that you are perfectly at one and at ease in your world and that you are totally accepted, just as you are. As you look at yourself in this world where no one is judging you, can you accept yourself totally as you are? Can you spot any judgments struggling to be heard? And can you put them away just for a moment? Can you see how flawed and vulnerable and human and beautiful you really are when no one is looking?

Can you see now how ridiculous this myth of perfection is? Can you see how deeply unfair it is to be judged against an unrealistic ideal and found to be lacking. Can you see how demoralizing it is to everyone? You need to tear down your acceptance of society's ideals and instead accept and welcome yourself and everyone for who they are.

In Japan there is a cultural value called wabi sabi which encompasses an appreciation of imperfection. This is symbolised in an art form where a piece of pottery which has been broken is mended with gold seams. It is deemed to be far more beautiful and of greater value than the original 'perfect' vase. And so it is with people. Those who have experienced life and its hardships, who struggle to find meaning in wisdom and compassion, who are brave enough to show their vulnerabilities or scars are truly beautiful.

The truth is that this is a beautiful world and you are perfect. We are all flawed. People come in all shapes and sizes, with our own stories, struggles, skills and talents. Beauty is found in the human spirit and we all have that inner perfection. We are all perfectly human, and so are you.

14 Letting Go Of The Need To Control

How small you are in a vast universe, yet inside your head nearly all of your thoughts are about you. Your mind is constantly busy seeking survival and satisfaction. What do I need to feel safe? What do I need to feel satisfied? You can spend your whole life busy and stressed and struggling to make the universe accommodate your wants and needs. You can desire the perfect lifestyle, like the one in the adverts and the movies, and you make plans to make it happen. You can spend all your time creating the perfect home, attracting the perfect partner, going to all the right places with the right people. But the harsh truth is that the world will turn quite nicely without you. You share the planet with 7.5 billion other humans, every one just as special as you. No matter how hard you want, or how hard you try it doesn't mean things will go the way you want them to. Sometimes they do, sometimes they don't and it is usually nothing to do with you. So let it go.

By all means set your intention based on what you want in the short or the long term, make the effort to get it, but stop grasping for the specific outcome your mind has created. There is no need to stress. Once you have decided what you want, and you are making the effort, let it go. Appreciate that it may turn out or it may not. If it doesn't the world will keep turning and after your initial disappointment you will find another way forward and life will reassert itself. It often happens that disappointment leads to a new path, a better one that is more fulfilling in the end. Roll with the punches.

I know this lesson sounds harsh but it is for three good reasons. Firstly, it is better for you to have a realistic sense of your own importance, no more or no less important than anyone else. We all have to live together on this planet of ours. Since you are not especially important you don't have to take yourself so seriously. You can take a more lighthearted approach to life. Secondly, there is not just one path to take. There are a million paths. Don't fixate on one way because that might just not happen and it will save a lot of struggle and disappointment if you can be flexible about your goals. And thirdly, it is better to be realistic about what you can control and what you can't. Really the only thing you can control is what you do, so focus on that. Put as much focus and effort as you can into what you do and get as much satisfaction as you can from what you do. Let this be what is important, and let the rest take whatever course it will.

Emma's story

Emma grew up a traditional family. Both Emma's parents were professionals with degrees and Emma's path was unquestioned. She would go to university and get her degree and get a professional career. No one questioned this, not even Emma. When she struggled with her GCSE's her parents got her a tutor. When she failed to get the grades at A level, she sat them again. She struggled through her degree becoming more and more disheartened. Her final result was dismal and her parents were not pleased. After an awkward spell at home with no job, Emma got a part time job helping out on a farm. It was quite a change but Emma loved it. She threw herself into it with such enthusiasm and energy that the farm employed her to do their office work and business development. If she had held onto her original expectation of being a professional she might have never felt the satisfaction of ending up in the right place, doing the thing she loved.

You see, when one door shuts another one opens. The new way is often a better fit for you, even if your original plans were different.

You might find that you spend a lot of your effort trying to prevent things you don't want. No one wants rejection or failure. So you work really hard to get things right, to avoid mistakes and gain approval. And you stress and worry about all of the things that could go wrong. Again, it is not within your power to prevent failure, and failure will happen. It happens to everyone at one point or another. You are lovely and good and worthy, but you are human and therefore you are not perfect. The only thing you can control is the effort you put in. Focus on the effort, be curious, learn, adapt and improve. Let go of the outcome because this is outside of your control and when the unexpected happens you will be able to adapt and move on. Let go of the struggle. Let go of the worry. Let go of the stress.

15 Letting Go Of Judging

Judging is something we all do, pretty much all of the time. It is very difficult to be neutral about anything. Watch closely and you will see that with almost everything you come across you either like it or you don't, it's either seen as good or bad. As human beings we are built to quickly assess whether something is safe to eat or not, whether someone is friend or foe. It's what your brain is built to do and it carries on doing it in autopilot mode.

We decide early on what we like and dislike and tend to stick with these preferences. This makes life easier so you can shortcut decisions because you know your own mind and what works for you. You keep these likes and dislikes clearly labelled in your memory bank for easy access, so you don't have to spend time assessing new things. Your subconscious mind already knows whether something new is going to be good or bad, friend or foe.

But these likes and dislikes and rules become like a straitjacket as you grow and mature. You can't explore something that you have dismissed. For example you might have written off classical music altogether, but maybe there are some pieces that you would like or even love. The more lightly you hold onto your likes and dislikes, the more open you can be to the opportunities and pleasures life has to offer, and the better you can assess when something is no longer good for you.

As well as personal likes and dislikes, judging also relies on having standards. It is like having a virtual rulebook. Without this you can't judge what standards you need to meet and therefore what other people should or shouldn't do. Some people carry big and heavy virtual rulebooks. If a lot of your thinking contains the words 'should' or 'shouldn't' you will know that your rulebook is big and weighty.

This sets you up for a judgmental approach to life. The trouble is that when you judge another person you create distance between you. You close down the opportunity to understand the other person when you decide that they are at fault. This is not a good strategy for building strong and healthy relationships with people. You never really know what someone else is going through so it is much better to listen and try to understand them. If you were to put yourself in their shoes you might be less tempted to judge them.

If you try to work out and follow all of the rules of society you set yourself up for failure and misery because no one can achieve all of the standards set. The bar is set way too high. If you worry about the rules and standards other people hold you will feel under scrutiny and insecure as you struggle to work out what is expected of you. It is exhausting and demoralising.

We accept the rules without challenging whether they are real, whether we agree with them or whether they are realistic. They are not absolute truths and if you study another culture you will find a different set of rules and standards. Listen out for the standards you have unconsciously taken on board. Every time you hear the word 'should' either inside your own mind or coming out of your mouth, pause and challenge whether that 'should' is real and true.

Take charge and make your own rulebook. It could have many rules or just one. What do you think are the important standards that people should live by if we are to create a fair society? What makes a good life? What is your mantra for life? Set your own meaningful standards to guide you through life. Check in with yourself regularly to see how you are meeting your own standards, and reassess every now and then to see if these standards still hold true for you.

Now you can start using yourself as a guide, rather than looking to other people or outside standards. You start to develop an inner certainty about what is right and wrong, good and bad and let the meaningless standards fall away. You stop worrying about what other people think of you and start to be more concerned about what you are thinking of you. Since you now have a clear moral compass you can rely on yourself to judge whether your behaviour, and the behaviour of others, is in line with that or not.

16 Detaching From The Ups And Downs Of Life

It sounds like such a cliché to say that everyone has good days and bad days but it is also true. If we could deeply believe that this is always going to be true, no matter what we try to do to fix it, we can relax and go with the flow.

Everyone has a share of good times and bad times. Life is a series of peaks and troughs from start to finish, with plateaus of normality in between. If you spend your life grasping after the peaks and running away from the troughs, it won't make much difference to what actually happens. The effort is pointless and will make you miserable as you cannot control life's events and the bad times will still come and the good times will still pass. Events that you judge to be good or bad will rise and fall in an endless wave throughout your life.

Difficulties, failures, loss and grief are an inevitable part of human life. They hurt like hell and you want to be the one who sails through a charmed life without ever encountering them but you can't. They come, but they come with important lessons. These tough times teach you what strategies you need to develop, what strengths you have to draw on, and how to care for and support other people when they are dealing with life's hardships. As you learn these lessons you mature and grow, developing strength, resilience and confidence that you know how to deal with difficulties when they arise.

The success, the windfall, the love of your life will all come along at some point and you will feel uplifted and euphoric and rightly so. You will want this feeling to last forever. But it doesn't work like that. After a period of time you get used to the new success or the new love and things settle back to normal. Some new difficulty will present itself soon enough and the cycle starts again. It is inevitable.

If you attach your happiness to the events and circumstances in your life you will swing from highs to lows as events around you unfold. Your happiness is at the mercy of things you cannot control. You are like a puppet where life is pulling your strings and you are not in control of your own self. You will always be chasing a new love, more money or more recognition. Sometimes you get what you want and sometimes you don't, and when you do get what you want you soon want more. Living like this is exhausting and inevitably disappointing.

Help yourself to steady your course through life by accepting and not fighting the fact that there will be highs and lows. Welcome the good times without clinging to them. Accept the bad times, knowing that they will pass. Write yourself a letter when you are in a good times, reminding yourself of what you need to remember when you are down, to provide comfort and reassurance to help you through the dark times.

Finding a way to be more or less content with life through its ups and downs means finding a pathway direct to the source of happiness, which means finding a way to manage your own state of mind. This means letting go of your belief that anything out there will bring you lasting happiness and realising that the only source of happiness is your own mind. Only then can you turn your attention to the real task of life, learning to be happy come what may.

17 Freeing Yourself From Being Judged

Every person is born into a distinct place and time. We each have our place in the history and the geography of the world. Each time and place has it's own culture, it's own set of beliefs, habits and priorities which influence all of the people that live within its boundaries. As we grow and learn about the world, we accept these beliefs and habits and priorities as if they are the truth, because everyone around us talks and moves within these cultural assumptions. We have nothing to compare them to. It is like a fish being unaware that it is swimming in water. It doesn't know that water exists until it is fished out into the air.

You are born in this time in this place and most of the people and leaders around you share a worldview. Understand that this shared view is just one way of looking at the world. Look at other cultures to find different worldviews so that you can more clearly see the values and goals that you have taken for granted.

In the modern Western world we have a culture that is dominated by a rational, progress oriented mindset. We praise and reward individual effort and achievement. Money is the goal. We have to suppress our natural, human emotions and fears in order to be accepted. We have to pretend to be rational, logical and confident. We have to be productive and always improving ourselves, instead of settling happily with what we have and who we are. We have to strive to work harder and struggle to achieve more wealth to prove that we are valuable instead of accepting our intrinsic value as a human being. And we have to do this on our own, without asking for help.

As we suppress important parts of who we are so that we can fit in and be accepted in our culture we start to hide these parts from ourselves as well. We pretend to ourselves that we are not stressed from over-achievement, not disillusioned with the emptiness of wealth as a goal. We struggle alone and pretend that we don't feel lonely or need company and support of others. This splitting off of important parts of who we naturally are as human beings is harmful to our mental health and wellbeing. Inside we are scared of being found out to be lazy, stupid, needy or weird. We are driven towards behaviours that distract us and numb the hurt and shame we feel inside.

Some of these avoidance behaviours are socially acceptable, such as being chronically busy. This helps us to avoid facing the pain of not fitting in, whilst also driving us to achieve more so it looks like winning. Consumption of alcohol or drugs, overeating, shopping and gambling addictions all numb us so we don't feel the pain that lingers underneath.

This is when self-acceptance becomes essential in order to be happy. Self-acceptance becomes a quiet act of rebellion against a culture that is trying to mould you to be a certain way. By accepting yourself you decide that you are just fine the way you are, you don't need to struggle to have or achieve what society dictates. You don't need to look or act, or speak a certain way. You can be honest about who you are. You can have your own set of values, likes, dislikes and priorities. You can follow your own path. It takes courage and support from like-minded people. It is the path to a life less travelled but well lived. It is the path to a happy life.

18 Freeing Yourself From The Pressure Of Time

When you are going somewhere and you have plenty of time, you can relax and enjoy the journey. When you are in a rush it is a completely different experience isn't it? You feel tense and uptight, you feel the urge to move faster, your mind races to the consequences of arriving late. The same journey feels completely different because your mindset is different.

It is easy and common for rushing about to become a way of life. We feel that we ought to pack our lives with activity. Some people boast about how busy they are and wear this as a badge of honour. And we can get sucked into the idea that busyness is good and praiseworthy. It is not. Being busy for the sake of it is not praiseworthy, quite the opposite.

Spending your life in a rush does not help you to live well because you don't allow yourself time to think. You don't have time to stop and consider if what you are doing is good and right or if there is a better way of doing things. You don't allow yourself the necessary time it takes to do the work you have to do. You don't give yourself time to reflect on what you have done to see if it was valuable and if improvements could be made.

When you are always focused on what you have to do next you are likely to miss what is really important. You find it hard to give the people you care about your full attention and you miss the chance for connection. You make plans about how to get everything done, not about how to get more out of life. Even the moments that you have planned to be enjoyed cannot be enjoyed, because you can't surrender to the moment when you are always thinking about what is next. You miss opportunities for change or growth because you are rushing through every task. You miss out on chances to offer other people a helping hand. And most of all, you miss out on the joy you can experience only when you are present to life in the moment. What you don't want to do is to rush through life in a race towards the grave, never having really enjoyed your life.

A life spent always racing through a long list of things to do is stressful and constant stress is bad for your physical and mental health. It erodes not just your enjoyment of life but your life itself. So give up the idea that busy-ness is a good thing. Instead look for balance. Balance between achievement and enjoyment, between doing and being, between speed and slowness, between a focus on tasks and an openness to life.

When you face obstacles in life you can practice your balancing act. Instead of getting impatient and stressed you can drop into your being mode rather than doing mode. Use the time to reflect and plan and remember what is important. Time spent waiting can be hot and impatient or cool and patient and you can choose which it is to be. Likewise, when people are not helping you by doing what you want them to do, cool down the rush of impatience and take the time to listen to their perspective and see if there is a way forward that all of you can get behind.

When you have time for ease and enjoyment allow yourself to fully immerse in the moment, drink it in. When you are with people you love, be fully with them, listen intently and open your heart to them. Don't rush these times. They are what really matter.

19 Letting Go Of The Story Of You

Your mind is a master storyteller. It jumps around from subject to subject, having opinions on everything under the sun, forming questions, worrying about what could happen, ruminating over things that have happened, hoping, wanting, regretting and on and on it goes. It never seems to tire or need a rest. Even in your sleep your mind continues to create stories in your dreams.

In the mind's attempt to make sense of the world it jumps on certain pieces of information that seem to be significant, and filters out the rest. It uses these pieces to figure out how the world works, what your place is within it, how to be in the world and what to do. It is constantly scanning for new information and adding to the storyline so it can form a consistent narrative – the story of you.

Your story of who you are, the type of person you are, your talents, limits and failings are made up by the mind from snippets that you remember, particularly from your childhood, from your life up till now. Your beliefs feel so strong and true but they have been built up from what a few people have said to you, and a handful of experiences. Their truth is much more flimsy than you think. And because our human nature is to focus on the negative rather than the positive your natural bias has led you to build your story upon only a few negative experiences rather than see the truth of the whole. Your story will be built on the failures rather than the achievements, the criticism rather than the praise, the worst rather than the best. And this makes life pretty miserable.

Because you believe your story, you make it come true in your ongoing life. You become a self-fulfilling prophecy in the story of your life.

Because your mind is so busy you are constantly in the grip of your thoughts and you cannot see that there is a way out of this treadmill. It is difficult to watch your mind at work because you are trapped in your thoughts with your mind on autopilot. To witness your mind at work you have to press the pause button and stop thinking for a moment and then you might see the thoughts and stories as they emerge. You might glimpse your mind creating a new thought before you get immersed in that thought. If you practice this pausing and watching you will find it easier to see your mind at work without getting caught up in the thought or story. And this ability is fundamental if you want to take over the autopilot of your mind. The more you do this the better you get.

You need to practice staying present to the way you feel as you go about your day. Whenever you feel anxious, stressed, angry, irritated, scared, shut down or any other reaction, if you pause and look you will see that your mind is telling a story. It may be a story of your failings, of another person's harsh judgment of you or a particularly gruesome outcome to current events. When you catch yourself in such a moment stop, take a breath, look at what is here and now, in the absence of stories from the past and the lack of storytelling about the future. In the space that you have created you will see things as they are, with many options and choices for what happens next. Then you can use your mind's wonderful creative storytelling capability to write a positive story of what you want to happen, and from now on you can write your own story.

Getting Through The Hard Times

20 How To Manage Anxiety

I know what it is like to struggle with anxiety. Your mind is on constant alert and your body is tensed as if it is waiting for a blow at any moment. It feels uncomfortable and exhausting.

Your anxiety has its roots in a deeply held belief that the world is not a safe or kind place and that you are not protected, so you have to protect yourself. This means being on alert all the time because it seems as though danger can come from anywhere at any moment. Everything has to be assessed for its level of threat. But you never feel really safe, because the next moment could bring a new threat. People that you know and trust might change overnight. The house could collapse or the sky fall down. You can never truly relax.

In our world most of the threat we feel comes in the form of social encounters. So every encounter is fraught with anxiety as each person is continually assessed; what did they mean by that, what does that look mean, why did they cut me off mid-sentence? Don't they like me?

You are highly attuned to the possibility of physical threat so you play safe. You take few risks and prefer to stay in than go out, to follow routine rather than try out new things, are shy about meeting new people and try your best to stay small.

Fear and anxiety are built into human beings so that we are alert to danger and therefore keep ourselves safe. The trouble is that this warning system is sometimes set to be so sensitive it makes our lives miserable. Then our fight, flight, freeze system is constantly on in readiness for danger. Stress hormones flood the system, muscles are tensed, breathing is shallow, the blood is thickened, digestion slows and our attention narrows to the source of perceived threat. This is not a fun state to be in and over time will damage your health.

To dial down anxiety there are a number of things you can do. Firstly stop fighting it. Accept your anxiety as part and parcel of being a human being. It is there in all of us. You can't take it out more than you can take out your liver or heart. Just like these organs it serves a vital purpose in keeping you alive and safe. So accept it – it has to be there.

Use your breath to calm your body and mind. When anxiety is taking over and your breath is fast and shallow, deliberately deepen your breath down into your stomach and slow it down. Breathe into where you feel the anxiety the most and gather it up and breathe it out. As you breathe out relax your body, and repeat a word to yourself like 'calm' or 'relax'.

Move your body so that it doesn't feel trapped with the anxiety. Stand, walk even if it's just to the toilet. Stretch your arms high, yawn. Get outside, or look outside and look at the sky, notice any plants or trees, feel the ground under your feet. Let these things remind you of the beauty of the world, of life. Breathe in a sense of beauty and wonder, and remember for a moment that you are a necessary part of this beautiful world.

At a time when you are ready, you can turn towards your anxiety with kindness and curiosity. Have an internal conversation with your anxiety; where is it based within your body? How does it feel? Does this feeling change with your kindly attention? What is it afraid of? Can you reassure it without dismissing its fears? Is there a way the two parts of you can work together so that your anxiety feels heard, and you can stay in charge of your life?

It is important that you make peace with your

fear and anxiety since you can't leave them behind. Over time, as you accept your anxiety and it feels listened to, bit by bit it will loosen its grip on you. You will be able to push yourself further, face new challenges and live more fully.

21 How To Manage Low Self-Worth

When you struggle with low self-worth you feel defective, that you are not as good or worthy as everyone else. You believe that everyone else knows how life works, except you. You think there is some secret knowledge that everyone else has, but you don't, and you don't know who to ask, or even what to ask. You can't even ask because asking would expose your lack of this shared understanding.

A lack of self-worth can be crippling. You try to avoid being seen. You can't say what you think. Your brain scrambles as self-doubt crowds into your mind. Because you think you don't understand life in the same way as everyone else, you cannot speak your mind for fear of being exposed with your defective self on view for everyone to laugh at or despise.

Your thoughts and the words you say to yourself are so harsh, so self-critical. You tell yourself you are deeply unattractive, boring, embarrassing, stupid, lazy ... the list would go on and on. You believe all of these things about yourself.

These thoughts, beliefs and feelings are so entrenched already that they torment your everyday existence. They leave you no peace. It's like they have created a desert where any compliment, a smile, an achievement is like a drop of water that hits the sand and instantly drains away. Nothing anyone can do or say will have any lasting effect to lift you out of this state of self-loathing.

And this makes you vulnerable. Your desire for approval and affection makes you an easy target. If people can see that you won't say no, that you won't risk offending anyone, they can take advantage of you and ask too much of you. You can't be assertive and look after your own needs when it is more important to be liked. You are a good person and you are equal to everyone around you and you deserve to be treated as an equal.

You are not seeing how brave you are. How you carry on trying to be normal when you feel abnormal, subnormal. How hard you struggle to make friends and connections. How hard you have to work to hide your anxiety and self-consciousness. How hard you work. You are not seeing what a beautiful, smart, kind person you are. You are trying to make sense of the world, how it works, and particularly how people work. You know that if you crack this understanding you will be able to fix yourself and help others. You are not seeing how smart you are, how your curiosity drives you to learn. You are not appreciating your determination to make something of yourself, that despite your self-consciousness, you want to be successful. You don't see how you always think of other people and how you put them at their ease.

So you need to start liking yourself. You have to turn inwards and challenge the underlying thoughts and beliefs. Every time you catch yourself thinking badly of yourself, stop. If you wouldn't say it to a dear friend don't say it to yourself. Look for evidence of your good qualities – notice when you do something well or when you show skills, kindness, intelligence or courage. Keep noticing and stopping the negative thoughts, and keep noticing the positive things you do and the good qualities you have. Make these your everyday habits until you learn that you are a good person. Gradually you will learn to accept and love yourself and you will be happy. And you have to do this work because you deserve to be happy.

22 Dealing With Difficult Emotions

It's completely normal to want to run away from difficult emotions like sadness, anger and fear. We all want less of the bad feelings and more of the good feelings. In your quest for happiness you try to push away the difficult emotions because they seem like the opposite of what you are looking for. It seems to make perfect sense to run away. Except it doesn't work. If you don't learn how to handle them they will keep coming back.

Anger, fear and sadness are part and parcel of being a human being. You, like all your ancestors, have these emotions built in and they are a human reaction to life, whether they are prompted by external events or internal thinking. You cannot ignore them, suppress them or run away from them because they are part of you. The only option left is to accept them. This is not saying to surrender to them, wallow in them and let them take over.

This is about turning towards the difficult feelings and allowing them to be felt.

Let's take sadness, one of the hardest emotions to feel. The sadness you feel could be a human reaction to one of life's events such as loss of a relationship, death or failure. It could be a reaction to life's situation right now, where you feel unsupported or trapped. Or it could be something that arises every now and then without apparent cause. In any case, there it is. Resist the urge to turn away and numb it out. Breathe deeply, relax and see what happens if you stay with the feeling of sadness. Go gently keeping an attitude of kindness. Feel into the feeling. Where does it hurt? Locate the place in your body where the sadness is felt most intensely, and explore what is that pain? What does it feel like physically? Can you breathe some comfort into the place where it hurts the most? Can you use your imagination to offer some kindness and gentleness to that part of you that is suffering? Does it ease? Does it intensify? If this gets too painful stop and relax your attention, deepen your breathing and relax your body. Bring your attention to your surroundings and do some normal activity instead. Return to the exercise at a time when you feel stronger. If you cannot do it alone, seek the help of a counselor. If you feel like you can't carry on with this burden of sadness, tell someone you trust or call the Samaritans or Childline. The truth is that no matter how bleak and hopeless you might feel, life always finds a way back. In the darkest depths of despair you will find the seed of recovery.

Anger and fear can be met in the same gentle way. They are inbuilt reactions to stressful events, based on the fight or flight reactions that have been necessary to ensure our survival. Now that we have become more neurologically sophisticated we can use our evolved minds to gain control of our impulses to fight or flee. To do this again you need to stay with the feeling, finding the place in the body where it resides. Use curiosity to explore the feeling. Is it hot or cold? Is it a sharp pain or a dull ache? What impulses does it create? What thoughts and stories are prompted by the feeling? Can you find out what is behind it? Can you see the essence of the trigger and response without getting lost in the story?

These types of exercises are critical to gain control of your emotional responses. You are using your conscious mind get familiar with your emotions instead of getting lost in the emotions. You are trying to understand where they come from, how they feel, giving them space to be heard and felt, and to gain an understanding of what triggers them. You are becoming an observer of your emotions instead of being swept away by them. When you are kind and accepting towards these difficult feelings and use gentle enquiry to gain a degree of understanding into why they are there, you start to tolerate them better and they become less painful. Difficult emotions will always arise as a natural response to life but you can limit the suffering they inflict.

To give you an everyday example, I might be shopping in a supermarket, busy in thought and accidentally bump into someone who lashes out at me telling me I am stupid. I feel a rush of anger. My heart races, my body and face heat up and I want to shout back. In that same split second that I notice my anger rising like a heatwave, I also keep part of my attention on what is happening, as opposed to getting completely lost in the emotion. I see the other person, their screwed up face, the pain that I accidentally caused them and understand why they lashed out. I instantly calm down and apologise. The situation ends peacefully, and is quickly forgotten.

There are many instances that provoke us on a daily basis. Your willingness to engage with your emotions will reduce much of the suffering that comes with being a human being. Your ability to witness and master your emotional response will give you a chance to choose the best course of action, and this ability is the mark of maturity that will smooth your way through life.

23 Dealing With Difficult People

Some of the most painful life experiences are caused by conflicts or difficult relationships with other people. Human beings are sociable animals and we rely on a sense of belonging to feel safe. This is why relationships assume a great importance in our lives and why ruptures in relationships can feel devastating. We respond as though they are a threat to our very survival.

When you are caught up in this state of upset and overwhelm it can be useful to challenge your thinking about how important it really is. Let's say someone in authority has reprimanded you for something you have done. You feel panicked and sick. When you follow your train of thought it goes something like this. You think you have lost their approval, they will reject you and you will be cast out of school/work/home. You can't survive 'out there' in the world, on your own. When you trace your thinking back to the threat to survival you can start to challenge its truth. Does this one episode mean that you have lost their approval? Is it likely that they will reject you on the basis of one mistake? Would they go so far as to cast you out? And even if they did, would you really not be able to survive? Would you find other friends and authorities to house you and give you what you need? Can you think your way out of this panic and find a calmer space to think more rationally about the reprimand, whether it was justified, and how you can make amends. It won't be as bad as you first thought.

Sometimes people will be mean to you. This can feel threatening and we are likely to react with stress and fear or anger. Your system (like everyone's) is highly sensitive to threats from other people and you are likely to be swept away with a strong reaction. So let's get you prepared, because this is going to happen, because it happens to everyone at some time.

Work on your self-worth because the better you feel about yourself, the stronger you feel and the less vulnerable you are to the criticism of others. It won't feel like such a body blow because you know who you are, that you are a good person, that you tried your best. You might have made a mistake but so does everyone. You might not be good at this thing that they are criticising you for, but you are good at other things and no one is good at everything. You know you are not perfect and that's ok. When you hold this realistic view of yourself as imperfect but good enough any criticism can be considered more clearly. Now you can assess whether there is something to learn from the criticism, or whether someone is reacting from their own insecurity and just being mean to try to hurt you. You might even agree with their specific criticism, without agreeing that this makes you any less of a person. Building your self-worth will help you to stay calm and be less reactive.

You can also bring your imagination to your aid when you feel you are being treated unfairly. Try imagining that you are like a stone. Any words, no matter what they say, bounce off, while on the inside you stay unmoved and fully protected. Only use this technique when you are being attacked unfairly. In an ongoing relationship it is not helpful to withdraw like this. You need to meet the other person as an equal to talk about difficulties and differences.

Sometimes, sadly, people are a genuine, physical threat and you need to be present and aware so that you can recognise when someone is getting aggressive and you need to get yourself to safety. Stay measured, don't return aggression, don't approach the other person and don't raise your voice. Just leave. There is no reasoning with someone who is in this state and it is not safe to try. Get support as soon as you can because this is a scary situation and you need to feel safe and be safe.

Remember, when other people act up, whether they are being mean or aggressive, whether they are shutting you out or being judgmental and criticising you, it says more about them than it does about you. They are acting out of their own unexplored emotional pain and projecting it onto you. Whatever they say doesn't change one bit of who you are, your experience, your skills and talents, your hopes and dreams for the future, the goodness of the person you are.

24 Getting Through The Hard Times

Sometimes things happen, bad things that can take you down into a dark place filled with sadness. You might feel torn apart, like your heart is literally broken. You might feel empty, inhuman with no feelings at all, just a bleakness that cannot be filled. You might feel that you have no energy to cope with even the basics of life, as though there is no point in doing anything. You may not know why you feel like this. You might think that you will always feel like this. Sometimes it feels as though there is no point in going on. Getting through these dark times is the hardest thing you will ever have to do.

You have to treat yourself as though you were physically sick or wounded, because it is the same. Be kind, gentle and patient with yourself. The way you are feeling is not your fault. Healing will happen at its own pace and you can't rush to feel better. In the meantime do what you can to soothe yourself. The rhythm of walking is soothing for the body and soul. Nourish your body with healthy, comforting food. Rest as much as you can. Read stories of people making it though hard times like yours, to inspire you and give you hope. Reach out to people who care for you and tell them how hard it is for you right now. Allow people to care for you. Wrap yourself in a blanket of kindness and as far as possible take refuge from the demands of the world.

Come back to the breath and let it help you and support you. Try to breathe more deeply using the breath to fill your body back up when you are feeling empty and depleted. Scoop up the most painful feelings and breathe them out. When waves of emotion threaten to overwhelm you, breathe out the sorrow, grief or despair. Cry it out too. Cry as much as you need to. Write out your feelings. Just let the words tumble out. See what changes you feel when you breathe, cry or write it out.

Talk to people who can help you. There are people who understand what you are going through, who have been through this themselves and want to help you. Look for charities, groups and organisations that focus on the issues you are facing. You are not alone and you do not have to go through this alone.

If you feel that you can't go on, if you reach a point where you feel that life is not worth living please please please seek help. Reach out to someone you trust and tell them. Tell your doctor. Phone the Samaritans. Find the hand that you can hold.

Know this. Every human life has dark times. Everyone has struggles, losses, sadness and pain. And there is always a way through these times, a way back to life, a way back to happiness. Always.

And when you get back things will be different. You will know what it's like to struggle and suffer. You will know that you can heal. You will understand when you see other people going through heartache and you will be the hand that they can hold.

25 Overcoming The Fear Of Rejection

Many of us harbour a deep-seated fear of rejection. Most likely this stems from an early experience of being separated, either physically or emotionally, from our parents or caregivers. To face the prospect of losing the care of your parents at an early age means that you might actually die if you are unable to care for yourself. This deep fear of rejection is linked in our early minds to a threat to our very survival. When our foundation of care and safety can no longer be relied upon to protect us we become acutely aware of our vulnerability. Because this experience scorches a track in our developing brain it is very deeply and strongly rooted and for those of us affected, it influences all our thoughts and actions.

For young children it is safer to assume that the

parents or carers are infallible because we have no choice but to continue to rely on them. No matter how poor the parenting is, how neglectful or abusive it is, most young children will cling to their parent anyway. It follows that if the fault does not lie with the parent, then they must be the one at fault. The child believes that he or she is causing the abuse or neglect, that they are flawed and reject-able. When these two undercurrents – the fear of rejection and the belief of the self as flawed – run deep in our minds and become our reality, everything is impacted.

If this sounds like you, you approach everything and everyone in life with awareness that you might be rejected. This fear drives your choices, your expectations and your behaviour. It prevents you from getting close to and opening up to others because you think that if they knew the real you then they will reject you. You fear putting yourself into the spotlight, so you take no risks, you don't speak up for yourself, you feel like you have no voice, nothing worthy to say.

You develop strategies to either make sure that everyone likes you and no one rejects you or that you don't get close enough to anyone to be rejected. In the first strategy you desperately try to fit in and not stand out, so you monitor social expectations and monitor yourself with minute attention to detail, obsessing over any minor mistakes or potential mistakes and imagining dire consequences. You try to please everyone all the time. You try to demonstrate how valuable you are by meeting all standards and expectations, caring about everyone except yourself and always presenting yourself in the best possible light. This is exhausting and ultimately unsatisfying because you never get your own needs met. You may not even know what you need or want because you block out that awareness in case what you find is unacceptable and leads to rejection.

Or you may find ways to avoid getting too close to other people. You might become a workaholic or obsessive about some hobby or activity that means that you don't have to get close to anyone. You might find that you tend to take charge of people or situations so that they follow you with their obedience but you can retain your distance. You might have mood swings, display anti-social behaviour or pay little regard to your appearance to put other people off getting close to you. Can you see how this is a strategy formed from your childhood experiences, but is hurting you rather than protecting you? It prevents you from getting close to the people who could reassure you of your worthiness.

The fear of rejection does run deep and it is hard to overcome, but it is possible to heal with consistent and patient understanding and kindness. When you feel the fear of rejection rising within you, recognise it as an understandable response to your childhood and in your mind wrap your arms around that hurt child within, sharing words of kindness and support. Use your breath to anchor you while you relax and stay with the feelings until they subside and reassure yourself that your fear, although understandable is no longer needed to keep you safe. You are safe now anyway, whether people like you or not. If your feelings become overwhelming just bring your attention to your breath and your surroundings and rest until you feel safe again.

Find people who can accept you and reassure you and little by little open up to them. Take it as slowly as you need, being kind to yourself as you go and take note of your progress. This is hard and you need to give yourself all the encouragement you can.

Slowly and patiently, with understanding and kindness you can heal those early scorch marks. You can accept yourself as you are and learn that rejection doesn't diminish you in any way. Gradually, you can step into the light and show the world who you really are, you can find the closeness in relationships that you really want and create the life that you dream of.

26 Releasing The Burden Of Shame

We live in a world where only the shiny happy parts of our lives are on show. Our fear of rejection is so strong that almost no one confesses to flaws and mistakes, unless they are carefully calculated to be right on the edge of being ok really. This reluctance to show and share our insecurities leaves us all feeling that we are alone with our deepest darkest thoughts, obsessions, histories and behaviours. We all have them and we all feel alone because no one shares. This drives us into feeling ashamed of these parts of ourselves. We all have a shameful secret buried deep inside.

You might have done bad things that may have caused damage or hurt someone. You might have done this on purpose or by accident. It may be public knowledge or it may be that only you know. You might have had something done to you that hurt you but you feel responsible, that you caused the abuse. You might have cruel or sexual thoughts about someone, or thoughts about doing something terrible. You might secretly do things to your own body. You might be hiding a tortured sense of your own inadequacy.

Carrying a sense of shame is like carrying a heavy weight and it might feel as though you need to be punished in order to pay the price of what you have done or are doing. Carrying this shame means that you are rejecting part of yourself and it takes a lot of energy to suppress this and keep it hidden. You have to be on constant guard to keep it private, which means that you can't risk being really close to someone in case they find you out and reject you. So you end up feeling as though you are locked in a prison with your shame.

Know that you are not alone. Everyone has their own story of shame. Life is hard and everyone makes mistakes. Everyone has to deal with these difficult feelings and many people carry their secret to the grave. If you can fully believe that everyone is suffering like you are, you may feel brave enough to start to look at your secret and accept that it is just one part of your story.

Imagine for a moment curling up in the embrace of a universal presence that loves you unconditionally. This presence can see into your innermost being, it knows your deepest, most shameful secrets and loves you anyway. Imagine the possibility that even with your shame you are still a whole, beautiful and lovable human being, just like everyone else. It is a part of your humanity. How does that feel? Whenever you feel tortured by shame you can take yourself to this presence and rest your pain in the arms of a loving embrace.

If you are feeling safe and if you have practiced being present with the breath you can do some internal work to loosen the grip of shame. When you are calm and settled with your attention on your breath, gently turn your attention to the shameful feelings. Focus on where in the body it is held, how does it physically feel, what emotions arise as you look there? Breathe into this place. Can you see what happened, what caused you to behave the way you did? Breathe. Can you sense the pain behind your actions? Can you breathe into the pain? Go very gently. If at any time emotions come up that are strong and painful, bring your attention back to the breath and only return to this exercise when you are feeling safe and strong.

If you are able to visit the site and the source of shame are you able to see how it was a mistake or a response to the pain you were in? Are you able to soften your attitude towards yourself? If you bring a kind and friendly understanding to yourself can you move towards forgiving yourself? Can you allow for a possibility that you could in the future forgive yourself for what you have done?

One of things that makes shame so painful is that you have to keep it secret and it feeds on secrecy. Sharing your shameful secret in a safe environment where you will not be judged is the key to escaping from its prison. If you feel safe to do so, write it out. Write the story as you remember it, or as it is happening now. Write out your feelings, both physical and emotional. It can be very helpful to share your hidden secrets to a page. They are no longer only in your head and this brings relief.

The best way to bring shame out into the light is to talk to someone about it, as hard as this may sound. Look for a professional counsellor who is trained to provide confidential and non-judgmental support, either privately or through a charity. They will have seen and heard many shameful secrets in their work and they will not be judging you. They will help you process these difficult emotions and help you to see that you are normal and good right through to your core.

Once you accept and release your shame you will be free to show yourself fully, as you really are, with nothing to be ashamed of.

Taking Control Of Your Mind

27 Taking Charge Of Your Thoughts

We have been taught that the mind, housed in the brain is the very centre of our being. It is true that when you lose your mind you lose your sense of self, and if your brain is badly damaged there is a very good chance that you will die. However if you stop thinking for a moment you still exist. There is a you beyond your thoughts. Who is this you?

We almost never see this side of ourselves because our minds work constantly and tirelessly generating thoughts. It goes something like this ...

[I look out of the window] It's a sunny day .. I haven't seen blue sky for a while .. I should take a break and go out for a walk .. but I need lunch first .. what shall I have for lunch? .. S is coming for tea .. must carry on now so I can take a break later .. I must change my clothes before I go out ....

Thoughts run on like this in a constant stream

without pause. Many thoughts are boring details of everyday life and activities. Many thoughts are the same thoughts that we had yesterday and the day before. And yet we feel compelled to go on thinking incessantly as though we have no choice. No wonder we feel that our mind is the centre of our being, it never gives us a chance to pause and question it.

Thoughts can be very damaging to your state of mind. We are genetically programmed to think more negative thoughts than positive thoughts, and this bias makes us anxious and worried rather than calm and happy.

For example, when you have a big event coming up you may spend a lot of time worrying that you won't do well. These thoughts play over and over in your making you anxious, stopping you from sleeping and making you feel pretty horrible. Your thoughts have a life of their own and make you feel bad.

You may worry a lot about what other people think of you. When you are in the company of other people your thoughts seem to jump into their heads and you imagine what they are thinking of you, and usually it is critical. This makes you feel bad, humiliated, panicky and you want to hide. But these are your thoughts, not theirs. You are imagining what they are thinking of you. Your thoughts are ruining your enjoyment.

Stop for a moment. Stop letting your mind run in its own compulsive way and take charge. Tell it what you want to think about. When you notice that you are imagining that someone is thinking badly of you, stop and bring your thoughts to your own experience, what you are observing around you and what you plan to do next. Just like that you have stopped making yourself feel awful and inadequate. Or when you catch yourself imagining the worst possible outcome from an upcoming event, stop and focus on the next steps to get your best possible outcome.

It may not be easy, but it is possible. When you direct your attention to a positive thought, even if it is just for a second, you prove that you can do it. You can take charge of where your thoughts are placed. You can change your negative thoughts to neutral or positive thoughts simply by being deliberate about where you place your attention and how you use your imagination. You can choose to think positively about yourself instead of negatively, on a daily basis, on a permanent basis. You can shift the way you see yourself and choose to see yourself as good enough, as competent, as confident and resourceful, as worthy and lovable. You can choose not to focus on the worst thing that can happen but hope for the best that can happen. You just have to keep doing it. Imagine how different and how wonderful life will be when you take charge of your own mind.

28 Directing Your Attention

Your mind can only focus on one thing at a time and what you focus on can make you feel good or bad. You might be drawn to focus on bad things that have happened, mistakes you have made, or to worry about what horrible things could happen in the future. You don't need to dwell on the negative side of life. We all make mistakes and bad things happen. Life for everyone is a mix of ups and downs. Obsessing about anything is not healthy and is evidence of your mind doing what it wants. Continually thinking about negative situations and fears makes life miserable.

It might sound weird but you can take charge of your attention. Instead of letting your mind wander where it wants, you can tell it to turn to what is useful and beneficial for you. Imagine how much better you would feel if you could direct your mind to the positive things that have happened and to optimistic hopes for the future. Think of your attention like a torch beam that you can direct to where you want. Turn that torch beam towards the things that help you and make you feel good.

This takes practice. Just like you have to train your muscles to improve in exercise or sport, you have to train your muscle of attention in order to direct it to where you want. There are two parts to this training. Firstly, you have to learn to notice where your attention is. This can take time to master because you are used to getting caught up in your thoughts. It can take minutes, hours or days before you notice that you are obsessing and remind yourself to redirect your attention. You could start by setting yourself a series of reminders throughout the day to check in with your attention and notice where it has wandered. Secondly, holding your attention deliberately on a subject that you choose can be tough. Your attention wanders when it is weak and the draw of the negative can be strong and pull you back. For example you might need to really focus on a piece of work, or a problem that needs a solution. It might need time to consider it fully, but your attention is easily distracted. Through meditation you can train your attention to stay on one thing. The more you practice the better you will get.

Keep a list of things that make you feel good,

people that matter, dreams you have, activities you enjoy, places and scenes that move you and good things that have happened to you. Build a store of your achievements, your values and your strengths. Keep these lists in the forefront of your mind and move your attention to these items whenever you find yourself in a negative spin. And then get busy planning. What can you do to help this person to feel better, what can you do to move towards your dream or to build more of the activity you enjoy into your life? This is a much better use of your attention than dwelling on negative stuff that makes you miserable.

It is also worth preparing a few antidotes for when you catch yourself lost in negative thoughts. When you find yourself caught up in worry about awful future outcomes, snap out of it by focusing on what is the best that could happen, and bring that imagined future to life in all its glory. When you find yourself worrying about what other people think of you, switch your attention to what you see and think instead. What do you observe, what do you think of what is going on and what is being said, how does this sit with you and your values and what is your opinion? And when you are beating yourself up over some perceived failing, remember your list of achievements, values and strengths and focus on these instead. Turn your attention towards making a plan to use or develop your strengths and talents to make a difference to yourself or someone else.

As you become better at controlling where you place your attention you will take charge of your mind and your experience. You will no longer need to wallow or obsess in negative thinking. You can be free to create your own mental state and attain positivity and happiness whenever you want.

29 Using Your Imagination Constructively

When your mind is in auto pilot mode your imagination is unchecked and the sorts of things that it makes up are usually negative. You imagine that other people think terrible things about you. You imagine that putting yourself in the spotlight will end in humiliation. You imagine the worst things that could possibly happen and worry yourself sick. Can you see how this is a bad use of your imagination because all of these made up stories make you feel awful and prevent you from trying, from living life to the full?

Use your imagination to conjure up good feelings. Imagine that you are quiet and calm inside when you need to calm yourself down. Imagine feeling grounded and connected with the earth when you are panicky and anxious. Imagine that you are filled with light when you are feeling down and depressed. Imagine your heart is open and full of love when you are feeling tired of the world. Simply imagine being happy and fully immerse yourself in the feeling.

Use your imagination to help you feel better about yourself. Imagine people welcoming and liking you. Imagine yourself doing a good job with people liking and praising what you have done. Imagine that you are good at the things you enjoy and people appreciate your talents. Imagine things working out for the best. Get creative and daydream about how things will end in success and happiness.

You can imagine being an object or a person that has qualities that you want to develop. For example, if you are going into a situation where there may be conflict and you know you don't want to back down or give way, imagine that you are protected by an invisible force field. Whatever the other person says will bounce off the force field while you remain unaffected. No matter how nasty another person is to you, their words will bounce off you while you remain unmoved inside. Or imagine being someone with qualities you admire when you need a boost of confidence. Play with your imagination; adopt the qualities of natural elements such as the sea, a tree, a bird and see how it feels. Do you learn anything? Can you follow the sea as it cycles though all its moods? Can you feel the patient wisdom of the tree? Can you imagine the bird's daily fight for survival and sing just for the joy of being alive today? You need never be bored again.

Imagining how you want things to turn out can be a catalyst for the change you want to happen. Visualise it by making a picture collage of how you want your life to be in say 3 or 5 years time. You can tear pictures out of magazines or print pictures off the internet. Make a real life collage of these images that represent your ideal future life-style. Without holding it tightly you can start to make plans to help it to come true. Simply having made a picture of your wish for the future helps you to spot the right opportunities as they arise.

One of the most supportive ways to use your imagination is to imagine that you are held by a constant loving presence. Physically it could be anything or anyone you want it to be, or nothing physical at all. Whether you imagine this hard enough for it to become a belief is up to you. Feeling that support is very powerful, and the question of whether it is real is less important than whether it is helpful. Billions of people around the world have a faith and there are of course a number of different religions, but all of them are united in finding comfort in having a faith in something bigger than themselves.

This intentional use of your imagination is one of the most powerful ways to manage your state of mind. So use your imagination in a deliberate and positive way to enhance your life and increase your happiness.

30 Being Curious

Your mind loves to show everyone how clever it is. This makes life stressful. You have to learn a lot so that you can show off what you know. You have to defend what you know so that you can prove that you are right. You are closed off to other people's point of view when it differs from your own because it puts you in danger of being wrong. Somewhere along the way you got the idea that you have to get things right first time.

Life is much more enjoyable when you realise that life is learning. You need never again feel ashamed because you don't know something. Instead you can treat it as an opportunity to learn. You don't need to fear making a mistake because you know that mistakes are an inevitable part of the journey towards learning. Now you can relax and enjoy learning for the pleasure that it brings you rather than for the need to be right.

And there is so much interesting stuff to learn about. You can follow your interests and desires to acquire knowledge on anything under the sun. You can advance your knowledge through formal education or simply learn for your own pleasure. You can develop skills that help you manage your life at a practical level or enrich your life through creativity. Approaching life with curiosity means that you will always grow and develop. You will always be engaged with the world around you, and as a result you will always be interested and interesting.

Maybe you will discover a passion, something to which you want to dedicate a lot of time and effort just because it is fascinating. Find the experts in the field and follow them. See if they can guide you. They have put in the work before you and can fast track your learning.

You can approach your own inner exploration with curiosity. Be curious about your habits, why you do things in a certain way and why certain things make you react the way they do. Be curious about your upbringing and how that may have shaped you. Follow your curiosity and gain insight into how and why you are the way you are. As you learn more about yourself you can change and grow, letting go of the things that no longer serve you and developing new strengths. The better you know yourself the easier it will be to make your own decisions about what is right for you.

When you approach life with curiosity you are

open to the world. You bring fresh eyes to your everyday experience and question what, how and why things are the way they are. You open to a new directness in the way you see the world as though the filters built up from your need to know have dropped away and you can see things as they are for the first time. You open to a sense of wonder and awe at the miracle and majesty of life, of people, of the planet and the natural world.

31 Talking Down Your Inner Critic

The society we live in teaches us to be hard on ourselves. It sets us high standards across all aspects of life, and this starts from the earliest age. Everyone we know is part of our society - our parents, teachers and friends – and they all struggle to achieve these standards themselves, and happily point out the flaws in others, including you. We are taught that it is good to be modest about our strengths and achievements, so we dismiss them easily.

As a result you have learnt that what you do isn't good enough, you must try harder. Or worse, that no matter how hard you try you still won't be good enough because you are not good enough.

To protect yourself from criticism and rejection from others you learnt how to do this for yourself, how to criticise and judge yourself first so you don't get any hurtful surprises. The trouble is that you have become so skilled and accustomed to criticising yourself that you are hurting your self-worth. The inner criticism can be scathing and it can be relentless, leaving you no peace of mind.

Confidence is a leaky bucket. You can't fill up your bucket of confidence if you have holes in the bottom. The holes are created by the constant habits of negative commentary and self-criticism, which drain away your confidence and self-belief. No matter what achievements you make or what praise you receive, your negative thinking will undermine your sense of pride and happiness and your confidence will drain away.

You have to tune in carefully to the things you are saying to yourself. Listen carefully for the words that you use to yourself, the words that undermine your competence and confidence. They might start with 'You always …' or 'You never …' It might remind you of a past event that ended in embarrassment, so you shy away from trying a similar thing again. It might list your flaws to convince you that you don't have what it takes to do the things you want to do.

It is as though there is a voice in your head who isn't you. It is you but just a part of you, because there is another part who is reacting by feeling scared and miserable. We all have this inner critic. Listen for the words. Sometimes they are loud and clear, sometimes almost below our consciousness, but their negativity is a drain on your happiness and confidence. You have to make it stop.

You do this by turning inwards to face the critic. First ground and calm yourself with your breathing exercise. When you feel calm and connected to your breath, try to coax the critic out into the light of your awareness. Use your imagination to locate where they are in your mind or body. What do they look like? Do they have a name? See if you can ask them a question. How are they feeling today? What would they like to say to you today? If they have answers, listen to them carefully and you will see that they are misguided but trying to do the right thing, to keep you safe. If you don't get any answers that's ok. Your inner critic is probably a bit taken aback at being confronted and will try to hide. You can try again later.

If you get an internal conversation going, you can start to reassure your inner critic. You can explain that you understand they are scared and want to keep you safe, but you are now capable of taking care of yourself, that you want to try new things so you can live life to the full, that this is very important to you, and you will take good care of them too.

Keep being aware of the messages of self-criticism that bubble up from your inner critic. Whenever you find words forming that make you feel anxious or unworthy, turn to your inner critic, and reassure them that it's ok now, you are in charge, you are doing your best and that really is good enough.

21 Shifting From 'Me' To 'We'

Have you noticed how much of your thinking starts with the word 'I'? This process began when your early infant brain developed and started to realise your boundaries. You reached for something with your hands and started to realise that the hand is part of 'me' and the thing is not. When you were met with a 'no' you started to realise that your needs and wishes were not the same as your parent's needs and wishes. You felt separated and from this separation you started to develop a distinct sense of self.

From this point, you became fascinated with yourself. You explored the outside world to find out what you like and dislike and how to get what you want. You built up a picture of who you are using the world as a mirror.

You created an identity using labels and stories

to describe yourself. You learnt whether you are clever or not, careful or clumsy, nice looking or plain, good or bad. These labels help you to think about yourself. You know what sort of person you are, what personality you have. You can describe yourself.

Since you know who you are, you know how to interact with the world around you. Everything you encounter is related to you. You can't see even a piece of furniture without liking or disliking it, judging it as good or bad, wanting it or not wanting it. Everything you see is judged through the filter of your personality and preferences, so nothing is ever seen as it simply is. Everything you encounter is about you, every thought relates back to you.

But who are you really? If you were to question whether the labels you attach to yourself are really true, you would find that they are not as clear cut as they seem. You will find examples where they do not hold true, you will see that secretly you harbour thoughts and desires that are not in line with your identity. You will be clever at some things and not at others. You will generally be kind, but sometimes have cruel thoughts. Your likes and dislikes change and you change your opinions. There will be exceptions to everything you hold to be true about yourself.

Pay attention and you will notice more and

more clearly that the labels don't work to describe you. You have a little bit of everything in you, and so does everybody else. You have all the qualities and strengths, all the weaknesses that everyone shares. You have times when you have excelled and others when you have failed, just like everyone else.

Now you don't have to hold so tightly onto who you are. You don't have to hold onto the stories of who you are and how you are different. You are free to change. You don't have to prove yourself because you are ok as you are, just like everyone else. You don't have to judge everything according to the past. You are free to make choices of what you think is best moment to moment, and free to create the future that you want.

Remember that this is the same for everyone else, whether they realise it or not. Try to resist the temptation to label other people, especially unkind labels. People may have acted in a selfish or harmful way, but they still have the seeds of everything inside, both good and bad. Try to remember this and instead of writing them off, speak to the best in them and try to draw this out. It may work or it may not. In any case it is good to try to see people as whole, even if they don't see themselves that way.

Since you are a whole complex human being and so is everybody else, this means that you are the same as everybody else. This means that you are ok and everybody else is ok (whether they realise it or not). You are no different to anyone else and you are no more or less special than anyone else. We are all in this world together, fundamentally the same. What hurts you hurts other people. What is good for them is good for you. Knowing this, you might begin to loosen your grip on thinking that focuses on yourself and shift your focus from 'me' to 'we'. You might begin to question how you can be of service to those around you. It is the ultimate win-win situation because being helpful to others is one of the best ways to boost your own sense of wellbeing and happiness.

Creating A Happy Life

33 Living Life Your Way

Through the media and popular culture the society that we live in shapes the way we are. It tells us what to think and how to behave. It tells us what is important and what we should want. It tells us which qualities are good and which are bad and what standards are acceptable, who is in and who is out. Society reminds us of these things many times every day through our interactions in person and online, through media and advertising. It is hard to challenge these messages that we are bombarded with every day. It feels like they are true. But leaving them unchallenged turns you into a puppet of society.

Instead, decide for yourself what you want. Now this might be harder than it sounds because you have to challenge the things that you have been told are true. So just for a moment try to imagine that you reject everything. Imagine that you don't want a successful career, or nice car, house, family. You don't want to be popular or attractive or well-behaved. Imagine for a moment that you are an outsider so that you can see with clear eyes the way things are.

When you have a blank space, think about how you want to live your life. What fills you with joy and inspiration? What do you need in your life to be truly happy? What achievement would make you proud? What legacy do you want to leave behind you? What personal quality do you value the most? What values do you want to live by? What matters to you?

It is important that you take charge of your life, because it is your life and you get to decide, and you don't want to waste it. You have to be strong to stay true to your values and dreams so write the list and keep it in front of you to help you stay true to yourself. Life won't go according to your plan and you will have to learn and adapt as you go. Change the list if you need to but make it yours.

You don't have to change the world. Living according to your values is more than enough. And you don't have to be perfect. Try your best, fail from time to time, and then get back on track. You don't need to be liked by everyone. In fact, not everyone will like you, because no matter what you stand for, not everyone will agree that you are right. Just like not everyone agrees that the world is round. Do your best to be ok with that, remembering this is about you living your life according to what you believe is right.

If you live your life according to someone else's plan, or simply conform to society's ideals, you will miss your chance to be fulfilled. You will live in conflict with your inner needs and values, which will be tiring and unsatisfying. Value yourself and trust that you know what is right for you. Honour this life that you have been given and live it wholeheartedly, filled with purpose and meaning. Life is all you really have and it's yours so take charge and live your life as a joyful expression of who you really are.

34 Living Courageously

We often think of courage as an act of selflessness or heroism where someone has put their own fears and safety aside to save others or stand up for what they believe in. This type of outstanding act of courage is rarely called upon. But we can live in a courageous manner. We can try to bring an attitude of courage to our daily life.

Courage is often thought of as the opposite of fear as though we need to conquer fear to be courageous. But fear is a part of the human experience, as natural and unavoidable as hunger and thirst. Normally what happens is fear makes us feel so bad we want to run away from it, so we don't do the things we are scared of, we distract and numb ourselves from the horrible feelings, or we act out in anger because anger is easier to cope with. Courage is a measure of our ability to live with fear without running away, avoiding, numbing or acting out.

Learning to live with fear is a practice, one that is best learnt in baby steps. In the safety of your imagination with a focus on your breath as home, bring to mind a situation that causes you mild anxiety. It might be a difficult conversation, a request that you fear will be turned down, a challenge that you are putting off or a boundary that you want to put in place. Whatever the situation is, as you bring it to mind notice the way you feel in your body, notice your breath, how your heart feels, how your stomach feels and any areas of tension. Stay for a moment with these feelings and see if they change under your observation. Then while you are inwardly observing your feelings, breathe a little deeper and just see if you can relax your body a bit, say 10% or 20%. Then if you are ready, revisit the scene in your imagination, taking your breathing and relaxation in with you. Can you relive the scene in your imagination with a slightly more relaxed body? How does that feel? Notice any thoughts that come up. Does your imagination conjure up fears of consequences, failure and rejection? Watch how your body and mind get stirred up in tandem as thoughts increase these physical feelings. Can you see this happening and challenge your imagination? If things get too much to cope with bring your attention back to the breath and relax. When you feel ready you can revisit the scene at a pace that works for you.

This is a tool that you can bring to any situation, real or imagined, for the rest of your life. You learn that you don't have to run away from fear or from the things that make you scared. You learn that these feelings that are unpleasant are also bearable, and the more you practice the more bearable they become. You learn about what makes you afraid, what is underlying that fear and you will learn to be less afraid, by degrees.

As you learn to live with fear and not run away you become better at facing challenges that you would have previously avoided and life becomes richer with experiences.

The beautiful thing about managing your fear is that you are able to live life on your own terms. You can speak your mind, you can express your feelings and beliefs and set your own boundaries with people. You can ask for what you want. You can act in a way that feels right without worrying so much about fitting in or what other people think. You become a fuller expression of who you really are. Ultimately, living courageously is living your own truth.

35 Living With Other People

Human beings depend on close friends and family for our survival. This has been imprinted in our brains from a long evolutionary past. It is no wonder relationships are very important to you. It is no wonder you spend a lot of time thinking about your close relationships.

Relationships are complex and often confusing. This is because a lot of communication goes on at a subconscious level in the emotional brain, which is too fast and subtle for our conscious mind to grasp hold of. When you have two people's emotional brains communicating with each other things can get unpredictable and messy. Relationships are both important and difficult to get right. So let's shed some light on what you can do to bring this to your conscious mind and in doing so get better at relationships.

Understand that your subconscious mind is tuned to perceive threat and is poised to interpret a tone of voice, a lack of response, a look or gesture as a negative response. You may be more or less sensitive depending on your early life experiences, your genetics and the particular situation you are in. It might take very little to trigger a stress response and you are not to blame.

The first step to getting better at relationships is to understand what triggers your stress response. Think about previous times when you felt uncomfortable with someone. Think through the experience, how you felt, and see if you can work out what happened to stress you. You can practice being more present to your body so you notice the moment you are being triggered. You might feel your heart race, you might feel yourself tighten up, as if ready to strike or receive a blow. You might feel hot or cold. Your chest might feel restricted and your breathing shallow. Try to bring awareness to these physical responses so you can get an early warning of when you are stressed, and become like a detective to your triggers. As soon as you notice that you have been triggered, practice deepening your breath to help calm you down and getting very present by noticing what is here now.

Secondly, you have a go-to response to stress which you reinforce every time it happens. Based on your habitual fight, flight or freeze response you will either leave the situation, attack or withdraw into silence or feel like your brain is going foggy and you can't think straight. These are deep learned patterns that your emotional brain follows when under stress. Can you work out which of these is your default response? When you calm yourself with your breath and being present, can you think of an alternative, more helpful response?

Spend time working out what triggers you and how you respond. Bring what is going on at a subconscious level into your conscious awareness. Make a plan for the next time it happens. Be present so you can spot it as soon as it happens. When you feel yourself getting triggered, try to relax and deepen your breathing. Try to bring an attitude of kindness to both of you. When you feel the temptation to lash out or withdraw, pause instead. Ask yourself, is there a better option? Are you better off calmly standing your ground? Can you calmly share what you are feeling? Can you voice what is going on between the two of you? Can you do this without blaming them? Can you let go of your assumptions of what they are thinking or what they mean and ask for clarity instead? Go easy, this is brave, grown-up work. It takes time so don't rush it. Give the other person time and space to adjust their behaviour in response to yours.

Sometimes it happens that the relationship gets worse as you start to be more aware and more assertive. This is because the other person is trapped in their default stress response and your change is triggering them. Stay true to yourself and your development, even if they can't join you. This is your path to happiness and in any relationship worth having the other person will ultimately wish the best for you.

If on the other hand, the other person is trying to put you down, make you feel ashamed, blaming you for what's wrong in the relationship or threatening you, you need to put a safe distance between you. You need to talk to people who can support you in creating this distance so that you feel safe.

Every close relationship needs tending. When difficulties arise it takes calmness and courage to be open and honest and to keep seeing the other person as the kind, whole person that you respect or love, whilst holding yourself in equal respect and love. This is the key to healthy close relationships that grow and deepen over time. These are the types of relationships that we all need to be happy.

36 Doing What You Love

It is good and right to be happy. When you are happy it is easier to make the most of your life. With this in mind you can happily set yourself the task of finding and doing the things that make you happy.

You can start off by finding happiness in the little things that you do every day. If you whizz through your day, you might miss the joy that can be found in the everyday stuff of life. When you wake up you can jump out of bed or you can take full pleasure in the warmth and comfort of your bed for a moment or two. You can hurry through your morning shower thinking of the day ahead or you can choose to relish the feel of the warm water, the scent of your shampoo, the joy of being clean. You can savour your morning tea or coffee instead of slurping it down while checking your phone. All of these simple daily pleasures are there to be enjoyed but can be so easily missed.

You can look for the beauty in your everyday life. Notice the weather and be grateful for its blessings, whatever it is. Notice the buildings, the sky, any trees, plants, animals you pass as you go about your daily life. Enjoy seeing a smile one someone's face. Smile too. Appreciate the feel of movement as you walk, the strength and ease that you enjoy, the feel of solid ground under your feet and the rhythm of your steps. And enjoy your rest when it comes.

Make a list of all the little things that you enjoy to remind yourself to appreciate them. Make a list of the activities that you enjoy, that give you pleasure. Are they creative or physical activities? Is your best time spent with other people socializing or are you happiest spending time quietly in your own company? What are the things that you love to do, that enhance your life and make it richer? It is your life and you get to choose how to spend it.

Think about the things that you haven't tried yet, that you think you might really enjoy. There are so many things that you can learn about. The more subjects you know about and the more skills you have the more interesting and rich your life will become. The more you do and learn the more opportunities will open up for you. Draw up a list of things that you want to try or learn about, and make plans so that they happen. And keep that list alive as new ideas come to you. Enjoying a variety of activities will help to bolster you when times get tough.

Try to find some activities and practices that help you to stay healthy and develop your peace of mind. They also have to be things you enjoy or you are unlikely to keep them up. Things like walking and yoga are good for both body and mind. Almost all psychologists and ancient traditions agree that a regular meditation practice is good for mental health. Learn about and put into practice good nutrition to nourish the body and mind.

Be aware that some of the things that bring instant pleasure are bad for you and lead to real misery later on. Anything that is pleasurable but harmful to the body means that it is too high a price to pay. Be very wary of any substance that gives an instant high. It will deplete your brain of the chemicals it needs for you to feel real happiness. It is really not worth it, not now you know how to create real, lasting happiness on your own.

Overall, try to bring some balance to your life. Balance activity with rest. Find your happy balance of social vs me-time. Find a balance between the time you spend looking after yourself and your needs and wants, and looking after other people. One of the greatest pleasures in life is making a difference to someone else, so help out where you can.

Prioritising the things you enjoy in life will help to ensure that your life is a full and happy one.

37 Being Grateful For Your Life

Imagine this day is the only day you have been given. In this single day you would drink everything in. You would see everything in its beauty and clarity, absorbing every detail. You would savour every mouthful and treasure every moment. There is enough beauty in this one day to last a lifetime.

You have tomorrow, and many more days to come. Because you know this you lose your connection and wonder, your appreciation and gratitude for the gloriousness of this day. As each day becomes much like the last you become bored and take so much for granted. If instead you could remember to be grateful for all of the treasures that each day brings you would find the key to lasting happiness.

Look with fresh eyes at all the things in your life that you have to be grateful for. For your morning tea or coffee, for your bed to sleep in and the pillow to rest your head on, the fact that the sun has risen on another day. Be grateful for human contact, the friendly smile and even the criticism. Say thank you for the criticism and decide for yourself if it has value in helping you to learn and grow.

Remind yourself to be grateful for the roof over your head, for running water in the taps and for the food on your plate because not everyone has these. Imagine how much joy you would feel if you were given a tap when you had spent every day walking miles to get water. Allow yourself to appreciate and give thanks for the things you consider to be basic.

Notice the little things. The smell of fresh air, how comfortable your clothes are, the small kind acts of others. Notice and give thanks for all the little treasures that go unnoticed. Do this all day, every day so that you realise how much you have to be grateful for. Make a habit of giving thanks so that gratitude becomes your way of being.

Be grateful to yourself. Thank yourself for making it this far, for still being open to learning and growing, for still trying your best. Be grateful for your body, whatever it looks like and whatever state of health you are in, be grateful that it is still carrying you about and allowing you to do the things you want. Be grateful for your education, both the formal and the life lessons you have learnt. Realise that all of the mistakes you have made, all the painful lessons you have learnt have brought you to the person you are now. They were all an essential part of your journey so thank them too.

Feel as deep down as you can go, to the very foundation of your being, the strength and irrepressible gratitude and joy you can feel at simply being alive. When you find this wellspring you have found the key to a happiness that can be with you every precious day of your life.

38 Feeling Full Of Life

Have you ever thought about how being alive feels? If you stop for a moment and maybe close your eyes, what does being alive feel like? Feel into your being and notice any physical sensations such as warmth, coldness, comfort or discomfort. As you move your attention through your body, are there any tingles or vibrations? The physical body and its sensations are the foundation of your aliveness, not just at a practical level of keeping you alive, but the deep satisfaction of feeling alive is found in and through your body. By becoming more intimate with your body you will find greater joy in simply being alive.

Take time to regularly check in with your body and how it feels. You are listening to your body and so you are not judging or trying to change anything, but just using curiosity to feel the sensations that are there. As you practice you will start to notice more and more of the subtle sensations that you never knew existed. A whole world of inner sensations opens up. You will become more familiar with how your body responds to the world around you. Notice how your senses take in the world around you. Become more sensitive to the sounds, sights, scents, touch and tastes of your world, and notice how your body responds. How does a piece of music move you? How does the sight of an insect make you feel? Feel more scintillatingly alive.

How does your body respond to other people? Do certain people put your body at ease and others put you on guard? Pay attention to these feelings and acknowledge their right to be felt. There are no right or wrong feelings, there are no 'shoulds' or 'shouldn'ts', there are just your feelings as a human being in the world and however you feel is right for you.

As you accept your feelings you will notice more subtle responses and you might start to see connections and patterns between your emotions and physical sensations. You start to become more attuned to the way your emotional brain and body respond to the world around you in a way that you weren't aware of before. As you become more aware of this internal source of information you can use it to guide you, or you can choose to work with it. You get to choose whether to let your inner feelings guide your decisions or whether you want to overrule them. This is your life. Either way, you have become aware of the fullness of your being.

As you engage more deeply with your inner world you notice greater subtlety and complexity of your responses and connections to the world around you and the internal connections within you. Consider how this parallels Life on the grand scale. Consider how Life started as single celled organisms and evolved into the magnificent scale and complexity of our global ecosystem today. The nature of Life is to become more complex and integrated as it evolves. As you become more complex and integrated as a person you are evolving as a person and fulfilling your own life force. You become more aligned with the process of Life as you evolve, and as you evolve you become more fully alive.

39 Loving Your Life

You are a product of the universe. The atoms that make up the cells of your body were all forged in the furnace at the centre of collapsing stars. You are literally made of stardust. The foundational energy of all life on the planet depends on the energy of the sun captured in the cells of plants. You are quite literally sunlight. You are part of this magnificent whole. As you breathe in and out so the world breathes out and in. Life is a miracle and you are a unique expression of life.

Life could only begin on the planet because of a vast array of improbable conditions being just right. We are nestled in a safe place in the universe on a planet made of just the right stuff, with just the right orbit around a sun of just the right size. From the very first single celled organism through every step of evolution, through the survival of every one of your evolutionary ancestors, through the reproduction of every individual from one generation to the next, to the infinitesimally small likelihood that you would be brought into existence – here you are.

So there is no doubt that you belong to this world. You wouldn't be here if you were not wanted. You are an intrinsic part of the unfolding of the whole of the universe. You can rest from the struggle of proving yourself and be safe in the knowledge that you are invited and welcomed into existence. You don't have to justify yourself. You don't have to be anything other than who you are, right now. After all, the whole universe and all of time have conspired to bring you into being.

You are incredibly precious and wanted and loved. This whole world is wrapped around you, holding you and supporting you and willing you to be happy, willing you to be an expression of who you really are, willing you to fall in love with Life. Fall in love with the trees, the stars and the birds, the weather, the sky and the ocean. Fall in wonder at the beauty and the miracle of the existence of the world. Love being here to witness the miracle and never stop being deeply connected to and profoundly grateful for this unique chance to live. Fall in love with Life.

Your responsibility is to cherish Life in all its forms, and to be the custodian of your own life and happiness. Your work is to bring the best of yourself into the world with as much kindness and patience as you need, to cultivate your physical and emotional health as best you can. Your job is to go deep inside and listen and learn your true nature and make choices of what to bring forth and what to shelter within with care and tenderness. Bit by bit you learn what the world needs from you and how to offer this in your unique exchange with the universe. This is the work of your life, to love and be loved.

40 Being Happy Anyway

What is more important to you than being happy? In your time here on this planet you want to be happy, but it won't be given to you. In fact quite the opposite is true. Difficult early experiences and a society conspiring to keep you hungry for more, influence a brain that is predisposed to fear rather than happiness. Be happy anyway. Happiness is a state of mind and you own your state of mind. Now you know how to control your state of mind. You have learnt how to be happy. Now you can start the work.

Happiness is work. It means applying your mind to the task of being happy on a daily basis, on an hourly basis. It is more like doing happy than being happy. It means staying vigilant to the thoughts that arise in your mind and sifting through those that are leading you towards happiness and those that are leading you away. It means staying present to your experience so that you stay in control of your state of mind. It means choosing over and over again to turn your face to the sun and away from the shadows, to turn your mind to the positive rather than the negative. When you do this notice how you feel better, because when work makes you feel good it is easy to carry on doing it. This has to become a habit or it won't work and when it becomes a habit it won't feel like work. Over time it will become second nature. Happiness will be your normal state of mind.

As you get better at staying present and keeping your mind positive you will become more attuned to your reactions to situations that threaten to knock you off course. You will be more present to your reactions and able to step in and take control. So when someone says something hurtful, or when you mess up you can stop your thoughts from spiraling out of control with stories of how awful this is. You can pause, take a deep breath, and bring a kindly attention to what is happening and what is the best course of action even if that means there is nothing to be done.

Happiness takes commitment. It means putting happiness as your highest goal and staying committed to it come what may. Whatever knocks come your way you refuse to let your mind tell you stories of catastrophe, of failing, of rejection. Time and time again you turn to the present moment, to what is right in front of you, to where happiness can be found. Sometimes the loss is so great that for a while happiness takes a back seat. Even in the middle of grief happiness is still there for you when you are ready to turn back to it.

And remember, there is nothing out there that will bring you lasting happiness. Nothing that can be bought or held or experienced will make you happy forever. Only the work can do this. And when you are happy you can have anything or nothing, it really doesn't matter.

Now you know what to do. Now you can create your life on your terms. You don't need anything to make you happy so you can live as simply or abundantly as you choose. You can follow your interests and live according to your values. You are free to make your own choices. Choose to be happy anyway.

Reading Suggestions

1 Finding your calm inner space

Mindfulness

2 Being kind to yourself

Paul Gilbert
Loving Kindness Meditation

3 Using your breath to find stability

Thich Nhat Hanh
Samatha Meditation

4 Being present in your body

Yoga
Body Scan Meditation

5 Being present in the moment

Eckhart Tolle

6 How to meditate

Meditation
Mindfulness

7 Why it's not easy being a human being

Carl Rogers

Antonio Damasio

8 How evolution made you this way

Evolutionary Psychology

Joseph LeDoux

9 How your early life made you this way

Attachment Theory

Psychoanalytic Theory

10 Being you

Internal Family Systems

11 Being human is enough

Humanistic Psychology

12 Being happy

Positive Psychology

13 Letting go of trying to be perfect

Brene Brown

14 Letting go of the need to control

Relaxation Techniques

15 Letting go of judging

Phenomenology

16 Detaching from the ups and downs of life

Stoicism
Buddhism

17 Freeing yourself from being judged

Existential Psychology

18 Freeing yourself from the pressure of time

Mindfulness

19 Letting go of the story of you

Narrative Identity

20 How to manage anxiety

Anxiety.org

21 How to manage low self worth

Pema Chodron

22 Dealing with difficult emotions

Emotional Regulation

23 Dealing with difficult people

Assertiveness Training

Daniel Siegel

24 Getting through the hard times

Tara Brach

25 Overcoming the fear of rejection

Pema Chodron

26 Releasing the burden of shame

Brene Brown

27 Taking charge of your thoughts

Cognitive Psychology

Jack Kornfield

28 Directing your attention

Meditation

Executive Function

29 Using your imagination

Visualisation Techniques

30 Being curious

The School of Life

31 Talking down your inner critic

Michael A. Singer

32 Shifting from 'me' to 'we'

Action for Happiness

33 Living life your way

Victor Frankl

34 Living courageously

Susan Jeffers
coachingforcourage.com

35 Living with other people

Relate.org

36 Doing what you love

Mihaly Csikszentmihalyi

37 Being grateful for your life

www.happify.com

38 Feeling full of life

Transpersonal Psychology

39 Loving your life

Self-actualisation

40 Being happy anyway

Printed in Poland
by Amazon Fulfillment
Poland Sp. z o.o., Wrocław

60253809R00096